Guided by a Horse Workbook Series

Book One
What Horses Can Teach Us About Mindfulness

Stephanie Sawtelle

Table of Contents

This series is created in loving memory of my first horse Downey.
Downey, there are no words to truly describe
the presence you were in my life,
the meaning you gave to it,
the enormity of the patience, sweetness, and love you shared,
nor the impact you continue to have on me.
I love you.

"Somewhere in time's own space
There must be some sweet pastured place
Where creeks sing on and tall trees grow
Some paradise where horses go,
For by the love that guides my pen
I know great horses live again."

~Stanley Harrison

Foreword on the Evolution and Future of the Horse-Human Relationship

For thousands of years horses and humans have been in relationship with each other. Our relationship with horses has evolved throughout history in a way that reflects what we could gain from the horses themselves and how we could use them to achieve our goals.

Generally speaking, our relationship with horses began as a way to survive. We used them for nourishment, transportation, farming, and war. Although horses are still used in those ways, as time has passed we've become less dependent on them for those purposes and our relationship with them has shifted to focus increasingly on competition, recreation, and companionship. It is fair to say that the majority of horse-human interactions today are still focused on these aspects.

However, even more recently people are discovering that horses have come into our lives to help us in yet another profound way. They can be powerful guides in personal growth as counselors, mentors, and teachers of interpersonal and relationship skills, leadership development, and increasing emotional intelligence. These aspects of our internal development are just a small sampling of the vast teachings available to us through horses.

I believe it is in this latest step in the evolution of the horse-human relationship that an important shift is beginning to take place. We are coming from a goal-oriented perspective which focuses on what we can teach the horse to do for us and how we can improve him, and stepping into a process-oriented perspective which focuses on what the horse can teach us about ourselves, and how we can improve ourselves through our interactions with him. Integrating both of these perspectives is crucial in further improving and evolving our relationship with horses both as a species and as individuals.

This current step will open up a more mindful, heart-centered, and mutually beneficial platform from which to continue to transform and create our relationship with horses. Through the combination of our own awareness and real-time feedback from our horses we are given the opportunity to more fully become the whole, healthy, and empowered individuals that we ourselves, our horses, loved ones, and communities need us to be. In taking this journey of self discovery with horses we have the opportunity to be the change we wish to see in our lives, and we receive the gift of watching the effects of that ripple out into other areas of our lives.

My hope is that this platform will support the emergence of truly equal partnerships between horses and humans in which horses are seen as sentient beings. And, further, that each will recognize their own, and each others right to fulfill their life's purpose in the way of their choosing, as well as pursue co-created, respectful, loving relationships.

The Purpose of Guided by a Horse Workbook Series

There already exist many excellent resources available on riding, training, and horsemanship. Therefore, it is my purpose, through this series of workbooks, not to endorse a new technique for training the horse, but to turn the tables and help people discover new perspectives available by seeing horses as teachers, and then to encourage them to incorporate those discoveries back into their relationships with their horses, as well as with themselves, their loved ones, and communities.

The workbooks combine informative text, stories, inspirational quotes and pictures, guided exercises, and journal prompts to help you integrate the lessons on many levels.

It is my hope that the insights gained will improve horse-human relationships, initiate a positive feedback loop in the currently accepted horse management practices and training systems, and will ripple out to have a profound impact on the reader's quality of life and the lives of those connected to them.

How to Use this Workbook

This workbook is divided into three parts. Part one offers the information, ideas, and examples related to horses and mindfulness. Part two is a collection of guided exercises that create opportunities for you to explore and practice mindfulness while spending time with your horse. And part 3 consists of journal prompts that encourage personal reflection on how the information from part one, and the experiences from part two, weave together on a personal level.

Additionally, by using this workbook you are invited to join the Guided by a Horse private Facebook group. There you can connect with other people also using this series of workbooks, ask questions, and post about your own experiences. Message me through my Facebook page Stephanie Sawtelle, Equine Specialist & Personal Coach to be added to the group.

Tips for Using Parts 1-3:

Part 1

- Use this part to learn about the ways horses can teach us mindfulness.
- Read this part first to familiarize yourself with the information and ideas around which the next two parts are structured.

Part 2

- Use this part to create your own opportunities to practice skills to improve mindfulness while spending time with your horse.
- Review the exercises in each step prior to working with your horse. This will allow you to stay present in the moment and better connected to yourself, your horse, and your environment.
- Refer back to these exercises as necessary when working through the journal prompts in part 3.

Part 3

- Use this part to record and learn from your experiences.
- Before each session familiarize yourself with the questions in each step prior to spending time with your horse.
- Have a pen handy since many of the prompts are best answered in the moment.
  - Other alternatives are: having a friend read the prompts and take notes on your responses as you go (consider taking turns recording each other's experiences), or have a voice recorder or video camera running so you can narrate your experience in real time to later record in the journal.
- Note that the first 3 session's prompts are identical to allow you to become accustomed to the flow of the exercises and to allow you to more easily compare one session to another. However, starting with session 4 the prompts change to guide you into deeper levels of mindfulness and richer reflections on your experiences.

<u>Part 1:</u>

How can horses teach us mindfulness?

and

What's in it for you?

"Mindfulness is a state of active, open attention on the present. When you're mindful, you observe your thoughts and feelings from a distance, without judging them good or bad. Instead of letting your life pass you by, mindfulness means living in the moment and awakening to experience.

- Psychology Today

How can horses teach us mindfulness?

One way horses can teach us about mindfulness is by modeling the behavior for us. Horses, by their very nature, are mindful. Because they are prey animals, they instinctively keep themselves safe by living in a state of expanded awareness of their environment. This awareness allows them to attend to the needs of themselves and the herd as they stay alert to potential threats by continually assessing and reacting to their environment. If horses were distracted from the present moment by extraneous thoughts they could jeopardize their well-being or safety by failing to take advantage of current opportunities to meet needs or by failing to react to a potential threat in a timely manner.

Another way horses teach us mindfulness is through their reactions and responses to us in each moment of our interactions. Since we are a part of our horses' environment, our feelings, moods, body language, and energetic qualities are continuously being assessed by them and they are reacting to us according to how we are coming across in the moment.

If we are paying attention to the feedback the horses provide to us about ourselves then they serve as a barometer of sorts as to our state of being at that point in time. Because horses live in the present moment the feedback they provide to us is in real time. This means that as we change something about ourselves (our thoughts, feelings, emotions, body language, or energetic qualities) we may immediately see that shift reflected back to us by our horses.

An example of the benefits of mindfulness and this real-time feedback can be illustrated by this common scenario:

Tim is running late for a show and quickly wants to load his horse into the trailer. This trailer is new to his horse, it's darker than the trailer he is accustomed to and has a step up instead of a ramp. Tim is feeling pressed for time and, as a result, his muscles are tense and he has the feeling of a pit in his stomach. His mind is racing, thinking of the consequences of being late for the show and playing out all the preparations he will have to hurry through once he gets on his way.

His horse is giving him clear signals that he is apprehensive about this new trailer. He is hyper focused: head up, eyes wide, nostrils flared, muscles tense. Tim is keeping strong pressure on the lead rope attempting to pull his horse onto the trailer, ignoring the fact that the horse is feeling fearful. Right now they are at an impasse, each pulling against the other, neither moving in the direction they want to go.

Luckily, in this instant Tim's attention is brought into the moment and he realizes that he has options right now. He realizes that his own state of anxiety and urgency may be negatively affecting his horse's already fearful state of mind.

So, instead of continuing to pressure his horse onto the trailer he lets go of his racing thoughts, takes a breath, and relaxes the pressure on the lead rope. Tim decides to give his horse the time and space he needs to assess the new trailer. Because of Tim's decision to change his state of being in this moment his horse no longer feels like he has to brace against the pressure and resist loading.

Tim's attention to his breathing and release of tension is immediately reflected back to him in his horse's relaxation. Now that the horse is relaxed he can assess the situation, and take in the information he needs about the new trailer to feel confident about getting in. Simultaneously, Tim trading his anxiety and urgency for patience and relaxation has allowed him to show up as the trustworthy and calm person his horse needs him to be in a novel situation.

This example demonstrates:

- The benefits of choosing mindfulness.
- The way a horse models mindfulness for us.
- How your thoughts can affect your feelings and body language.
- How being aware can allow you to decide how you want to "show up" in the moment.
- How you may see your way of being reflected back to you by your horse.

What's in it for you?

Incorporating mindfulness into the time you spend interacting with your horse can be immensely rewarding to your relationship and an important skill to carry into other aspects of your life.

Learning to be aware of the feedback you're getting from your horse and yourself in each moment can help reduce stress for both of you and enable you to make appropriate decisions throughout your time together. You will be safer, the lines of communication will be more open, and the opportunity for harmony and joyfulness increases.

Furthermore, if you can be aware of the feedback your horse offers you about your state of being in real time, you'll become more conscious of the way you show up in your life on the physical, mental, emotional, and energetic levels. Being conscious of how you show up means you have more influence and decision-making power over that aspect of yourself.

Becoming present through mindfulness practice can improve the quality of the time you spend with your horse by preventing superfluous thoughts, baggage from your day, or concerns about your future from stealing your attention or negatively affecting your interactions and experiences. If your thoughts are elsewhere you may be distracted enough to miss important communication from your horse and available information from your environment!

For example, imagine this scenario: Beth shows up at the barn to ride her horse. She's already had a stressful day at work and is anticipating the time and energy it will take to care for her family's needs when she gets home. Her thoughts alternate between her experiences at work that day and her worries about coordinating the evening.

Let's consider two possible outcomes to this scenario. One in which mindfulness skills are used and one in which they are not:

Outcome 1: Because her thoughts are elsewhere, Beth doesn't notice that her horse turns his head away as she tries to halter him and that he is now pinning his ears and swishing his tail as she grooms him. She is going through the motions of preparing to ride but is not aware that her horse is telling her his back is uncomfortable because her mind isn't on the present moment. Because of his discomfort he doesn't stand still at the mounting block and is uncooperative during their ride. Beth thinks he has a bad attitude, blames him for an unenjoyable ride, and feels resentful towards him.

Outcome 2: Before approaching her horse, Beth clears her head of extraneous thoughts by bringing her attention to the present moment. Because she isn't distracted by those thoughts she is able to note, during her initial greeting, that her horse turns his head away when she attempts to halter him. She steps back, acknowledges his communication and waits for him to come to her to be haltered. This behavior is a clue to her that something may be off with her horse today.

Consequently she is aware of any further communication from him as she starts grooming in preparation to ride. When she notices the ear pinning and tail swishing she decides to look into possible causes for his discomfort. She discovers that he has sore muscles along the right side of his spine, assesses her saddle fit, and adjusts the padding accordingly.

Because of this adjustment her horse is more comfortable wearing his tack, stands still for mounting because the saddle is no longer hurting him, and is able to perform better while being ridden.

The result of outcome 1 is that Beth mindlessly pushed on into a ride which became unenjoyable for them both. If she continues in this way she may risk her horse's soundness, an enjoyable relationship, and escalating undesirable behavior from her horse.

The result of scenario 2 is that Beth attended to her horse's needs thereby strengthening their bond and she preserved relaxation and ease in their mounted work.

Another benefit of bringing mindfulness to the time you spend with your horse is you come to realize how your thoughts affect your mood, your mood affects how you feel, and how you feel is reflected by both your body language and the energy you give off. Horses are masters at reading all those non-verbal signals, so if your awareness is on the present moment you can avoid bringing in elements that aren't necessary, helpful, or relevant to the current situation. Being mindful in the presence of your horse allows you to assess and react to what's happening in real time both in yourself and in your horse.

In addition to mindfulness practices positively influencing the relationship between you and your horse, they can also be carried into other situations and relationships in your life creating similar benefits. For example, consider the benefit of really listening and being aware of the communication, verbal and nonverbal, coming from those around you, instead of paying attention to your own mental chatter. You will be better at listening and more able to give appropriate replies. You'll be more in control of how you're showing up in a situation, deciding how to be instead of constantly being in a state of reactivity.

Summary

Horses teach you mindfulness in two ways:

- **By modeling it, as it is their natural state of being.**
- **By providing real-time feedback through their reactions to you, which are reflective of your moment-to-moment state of being.**

The benefits of learning and practicing mindfulness in the presence of horses, *that can apply to both the time spent with your horse and in all other aspects of your life,* include:

- **Increasing your potential to experience joy, flow, and harmony.**
- **Having a clear awareness of, and influence over, what's happening in the moment.**
- **"Showing up" as authentically as possible in every situation.**
- **Being untroubled by extraneous thoughts or concerns.**
- **Having closer relationships and better communication.**

Part 2:

Guided Exercises

"Mindfulness is simply being aware of what is happening right now without wishing it were different; enjoying the pleasant without holding on when it changes (which it will); being with the unpleasant without fearing it will always be this way (which it won't)."

–James Baraz

Step 1: Arrival, approach, and greeting

1.   Mindfulness can begin even before you visually see your horse. As you arrive on the property where your horse lives take a few moments to notice your breath and check in with your 5 senses. If thoughts come into your head notice them then refocus on your breath and check in again with your 5 senses.

With practice and consistency the quality and duration of your mindfulness will improve. It may be helpful to set a timer or alarm to remind you at regular intervals to repeat this mindfulness exercise until it becomes more habitual for you. As this becomes more habitual you will more often be present in the moment and less distracted by extraneous or unnecessary thoughts.

2.   Whether your horse is in a stall, turnout, or pasture, monitor both your internal feelings and sensations as well as his body language as you approach and greet him. If you notice any feelings in yourself such as apprehension, nervousness, fear, or uncertainty do not ignore, minimize, or try to talk yourself out of them. Instead, pause in your approach and wait until you feel it is appropriate to resume. Keep in mind, these signals from yourself on how to approach your horse can come in the form of thoughts, emotions, feelings, and physical sensations.

   Likewise, if you notice any body language in your horse that expresses apprehension, nervousness, fear, or uncertainty also honor that by pausing until his body language tells you it is appropriate to resume. Keep in mind horses communicate (often in incredibly subtle ways) through changes in body language, posture, positioning, breathing, and expressions. Look for even the smallest signals such as a turn of your horse's head, a change in his breathing, or a shifting of his weight.

*IMPORTANT: Particularly if you notice any apprehension, nervousness, fear, uncertainty, or discomfort in yourself or your horse pause to consider the importance of carefully choosing the next best step for both of you. Ignoring or pushing through these warning signs may set you and your horse up for unnecessarily difficult, or fearful circumstances.

This is especially true if you are both experiencing them simultaneously. If this is the case, allow yourself to consider alternatives such as being with your horse from a distance or retreating to a distance that allows you both a feeling of comfort. Remain at this distance until you observe changes in the comfort level of each of you.

This method of approaching and greeting your horse shows awareness of, and respect for, each of your personal space, boundaries, and comfort levels. Through practicing this method of approaching and greeting your horse you are allowing for a mutually agreed upon hello!

3.   Using the journal to track your experiences with these exercises over the course of 12 sessions may allow you to start seeing patterns and making connections that may otherwise not have been apparent.

It will allow you to see more clearly how you initiate your time with your horse which gives you the chance to determine if you want to create that experience differently from session to session.

Step 2: Grooming and preparing your horse

1.   Take time to consider the location and preparation of your grooming and tacking area. This is a time for you and your horse to get a baseline reading on each other and to set the mood for your time together. Choosing a place to groom and prepare where you will have the fewest distractions, and where you are both comfortable and relaxed, will be most beneficial to allowing you to practice mindfulness techniques. Have your grooming tools, tack, and any other necessary equipment or supplies nearby so your horse is not left unattended and the flow of your encounter isn't interrupted by retrieving forgotten items.

2.   Before beginning to groom stand next to your horse and notice your breath again. Notice your own breath and that of your horse. You may choose to do this exercise with your eyes open so you can see your horse breathe or with your eyes closed and your hands on your horse so you can feel him inhaling and exhaling. Breathe with your horse and check in with your 5 senses. Stay with this exercise until you feel both you and your horse are ready to begin the grooming process.

3.   As you proceed with grooming reconnect with your breath and 5 senses at regular intervals. These intervals could be defined by setting a timer, by the change from one grooming tool to another, or by moving to each new area of the horse (neck to shoulder, shoulder to back, back to hindquarters, etc.). Use your imagination to come up with a reminder that works for you!

4.   While grooming monitor your horse's communication with you. Remember communication from a horse may show up (often in incredibly subtle ways) through changes in body language, posture, positioning, breathing, and expressions. Take note of any changes, assess what your horse is communicating to you, and react accordingly. For example, if your horse tenses and then lifts his head when you want to brush his face, he may be fearful of being touched there or he may prefer a different grooming tool than the one you are about to use.

In either case you can choose how to respond to what he is saying to you. In the first scenario you might choose to take small steps towards helping him overcome the fear. In the second case you may gently experiment with other grooming tools to find one he prefers.

Conversely, if he sighs, lowers his neck, and gets a soft look in his eye he may be telling you he is very comfortable with the situation and finding this activity relaxing.

5.   Repeat these exercises while tacking up or making additional preparations. Regularly check in with your breath and 5 senses, and note any communication you receive from your horse no matter how subtle.

An example here might be that your horse shifts his weight and then starts to fidget when you put on the saddle pad. If you ignore this communication it may lead to more intense fidgeting or even nipping when you saddle and girth him. But if you assess the situation at the first sign of communication you may decide your horse is anticipating discomfort or pain and evaluate the fit of your saddle.

6.   Using the journal to track your experiences with these exercises over the course of 12 sessions may allow you to start seeing patterns and making connections that may otherwise not have been apparent. It may allow you to begin noticing ever more subtle communication from your horse, as well as correlations between your own level of presence and the quantity or quality of feedback your horse provides to you about yourself.

Step 3: "Mane" event pre-assessment

Note: Use these exercises prior to whatever type of work or activity you plan to do with your horse. This includes any mounted or unmounted sessions whether they are for the purpose of training, practice, recreation, etc.

1. As you make final preparations or adjustments continue to practice mindfulness. Notice your breath and that of your horse. Check in with your 5 senses. Notice any communication from your horse at this time and as you make final preparations.

2. Take a snapshot of your present state of being. Consider your mood, confidence level, emotions, body language, focus, and thoughts.

3.   Take a snapshot of your horse's present state of being. Consider his mood, confidence level, emotional state, body language, and focus. These snapshots contain useful information in determining your next best step.

4.   As you are aware and mindful of your current state of being and that of your horse, decide if it is the appropriate time to move on to what you were planning for the session or if something else is needed at this time.

IMPORTANT: Particularly if you notice any apprehension, nervousness, fear, uncertainty, or discomfort in yourself or your horse pause to consider the importance of carefully choosing the next best step for both of you. Ignoring or pushing through these warning signs may set you and your horse up for unnecessarily difficult, or fearful circumstances. This is especially true if you are both experiencing them simultaneously.

If this is the case, allow yourself to consider alternatives to riding such as groundwork, lunging, liberty work, hand walking, or grazing, as either a warm-up to, or substitution for, riding.

5.   Using the journal to track your experiences with these exercises over the course of 12 sessions may allow you to start seeing patterns and making connections that may otherwise not have been apparent.

It will allow you to see more clearly what's happening during your time with your horse which gives you the chance to determine if you want to create that experience differently from session to session.

Step 4: "Mane" event

1.   As you ride, train, or work with your horse return to the mindfulness practices at regular intervals. Notice your breath, check in with your 5 senses. These regular intervals can be defined by setting a timer, by the change from one gait or movement to another, or by moving to each new area of the arena or trail. Or, use your imagination to come up with a reminder that works for you. Doing this will keep you present in the moment and can interrupt extraneous or unnecessary thoughts that distract you from the present moment..

2.   During your work take regular snapshots of your present state of being. Consider your mood, confidence level, emotions, physical sensations (most notably tension), body language, focus, and thoughts.

3.   Also, take regular snapshots of your horse's present state of being. Consider his mood, confidence level, emotional state, physical qualities (most notably tension), body language, and focus.

These snapshots contain useful information in determining your next best step and for troubleshooting when necessary.

4.   It's important to take note of the relationship between these elements, observations of your own state of being, and the circumstances of your work together when significant changes arise so you can start to see patterns and notice the components that contribute to ease and harmony or tension and imbalance. Incorporating these exercises into your session will give you a clearer awareness of what's happening in the moment and a broader perspective from which to make assessments and decisions regarding future sessions.

5.   Using the journal to track your experiences with these exercises over the course of 12 sessions may allow you to start seeing patterns and making connections that may otherwise not have been apparent.

Having a deeper understanding of the dynamics at play during your sessions will allow you to enjoy the moments of harmony and connection you have with your horse and help you see what may be blocking the flow in times of tension or imbalance.

Step 5: "Mane" Event Post-Assessment

1.   After you ride, train, or work with your horse continue to repeat the mindfulness practices at regular intervals. Notice your breath, check in with your 5 senses. As this becomes more habitual you will more easily catch yourself allowing your mind to fill with distracting, unnecessary, or unrelated thoughts, and be able to bring yourself back to the present moment through focusing on your breath and 5 senses.

2.   At this time take another snapshot of your present state of being. Consider your mood, confidence level, emotions, physical sensations, body language, focus, and thoughts. The journal will prompt you to reflect on how these observations compare to your observations from the other segments of the time your spend with your horse.

3.   Again, take a snapshot of your horse's present state of being. Consider his mood, confidence level, emotional state, physical qualities, body language, and focus. The journal will prompt you to reflect on how these observations compare to your observations from the other segments of the time your spend with your horse. Incorporating these exercises into your post-session time will give you a clearer awareness of what's happening in the moment and a broader perspective from which to make assessments and decisions on future interactions with your horse.

4.   Take a moment to thank your horse for his effort and participation after your work together. Consider how you can show him you appreciate your time together. This might be a special treat, a scratch in his favorite itchy spot, or spending a few more moments just being together.

5.   Using the journal to track your experiences with these exercises over the course of 12 sessions may allow you to start seeing patterns and making connections that may otherwise not have been apparent.

Step 6: Life Applications

1.   Consider how what have you learned or experienced through these exercises with your horse can be helpful in other areas of your life. These skills can be applied to relationships, family, work, school, social groups, sports, hobbies, and in countless other areas.

2.   Some applications of mindfulness or some parts of these exercises may come easier to you than others. It is best to pick one application, skill, or exercise that you feel most comfortable with to start applying to a situation outside of time spent with your horse. Do your best to approach this integration with openness and curiosity and allow yourself to experience the outcome without judgement.

3.   Challenge yourself to bring increasing levels of mindfulness into all areas of your life. The more you practice the more habitual it will become. You will begin to notice how being mindful benefits you and you may even notice that your own mindfulness has positive effects on those with whom you spend time.

Part 3:

Journal Prompts

Hold your horses!
First, a few warm up questions.

"Wherever you are, be all there."
-Jim Elliot

Date: _____ Time: _____

Additional notes:

_____

_____

_____

_____

1.   What prompted you to use this journal?

_____

_____

_____

_____

2.   What do you hope to gain or learn from using this journal?

_____

_____

_____

_____

3.   Describe your current understanding of mindfulness.

_____

_____

_____

_____

4.   What issues are you currently experiencing that you hope to get clarity on or find solutions for?

_____

_____

_____

_____

5.   What questions do you have about your horse, your techniques, or the time you spend with your horse that you hope to find guidance for by using this journal?

_____

_____

_____

_____

6.   What questions do you have about your relationships, family, friends, work, career, school, life, etc that you hope to find guidance for by using this journal?

_____

_____

_____

_____

Session 1

"**The way you get to know yourself is by the expression on other people's faces.**"
- Gil Scott Heron

Date: _____ Time: _____

Additional notes:

_____

_____

_____

_____

Step 1: Arrival, approach, and greeting

*For additional guidance reference Part 2, Step 1

1.   Upon arrival to where your horse is kept, check in with your breath and 5 senses. How would you describe your breath? What do you see? Hear? Smell? Taste? Feel?

_____

_____

_____

_____

2.   Describe your experience with this first exercise? How is this different from your usual arrival to where your horse lives?

_____

_____

_____

_____

3. As you approach your horse what do you notice in yourself? Describe any feelings, sensations, or emotions you experience as you approach your horse. Do they change or stay the same? How do you react to them?

_____

_____

_____

_____

4. How is your horse reacting to you? Describe any communication coming from him in the form of body language, posture, positioning, breathing, and expressions. Does he change or stay the same? How do you react to him?

_____

_____

_____

_____

5. When and how do you greet your horse? When and how does he greet you?

_____

_____

_____

_____

6. How does this differ from the usual way you approach and greet your horse?

_____

_____

_____

_____

Step 2: Grooming and preparing

*For additional guidance reference Part 2, Step 2

1. What do you notice about your preparation area? Is there anything you would like to have or do differently? If so, what steps can you take to make those changes?

_____

_____

_____

_____

2. Describe the experience of breathing with your horse. What benefit does this exercise give you? How does your horse react to synchronized breathing?

_____

_____

_____

_____

3. How often do you repeat the mindfulness exercises of noticing your breath and checking in with your 5 senses? What affect does this have on keeping you present and aware of your environment and horse? What other sensations, feelings, emotions, or thought patterns do you notice while checking in with yourself?

_____

_____

_____

_____

4. While grooming and preparing your horse, what communication(s) do you receive from him in the form of changes in body language, posture, positioning, breathing, and expressions? What is occurring that causes your horse to express this to you? What might he be communicating to you?

_____

_____

_____

_____

5. At the time of this communication what do you notice in yourself as far as feelings, sensations, emotions, or thoughts? What would you like to do as a result of this communication?

_____

_____

_____

_____

6. What, if any, changes would you or your horse like to make in the grooming and preparation process? What steps do you need to take to make those changes? What might be the result of those changes?

_____

_____

_____

_____

Step 3: "Mane" event pre-assessment

*For additional guidance reference Part 2, Step 3

1.   As you make final preparations or adjustments what do you notice about your breath? About your horse's breath? What is registering in each of your 5 senses?

_____

_____

_____

_____

2.   Describe your mood, confidence level, emotions, body language, focus, and thoughts. What effect, if any, are these having on your horse?

_____

_____

_____

_____

3.   Observe your horse. Describe his mood, confidence level, emotional state, and focus. Challenge yourself to base these observations on his body language, expression, and posture to avoid projecting. What effect, if any, are these having on you?

_____

_____

_____

_____

4.   What communications are you getting from your horse as you make final preparations to ride?

_____

_____

_____

_____

5.   Based on your observations of your own and your horse's current states of being, what is the next best step to take?

_____

_____

_____

_____

6.   What, if anything, would you like to be experiencing differently right now? What steps can you take to make your pre-ride experience better for you and/or your horse?

_____

_____

_____

_____

Step 4: "Mane" event

*For additional guidance reference Part 2, Step 4

1.   How are you reminding yourself to stay present, notice your breath, and check in with your 5 senses? Describe the effect these reminders are having on your level of presence and ability to stay in the moment. How often do these reminders interrupt unnecessary thoughts, a negative mental tape-loop, or worries about the future?

_____

_____

_____

_____

2.   Use the following chart to track notable circumstances, changes, or events (positive or negative). With each circumstance note your mood, confidence level, emotions, physical sensations (most notably tension), body language, focus, and thoughts. Also note your horse's mood, confidence level, emotional state, physical qualities (most notably tension), body language, and focus. Then record any correlations or patterns you see developing.

Notable circumstance.	Notes on your mood, confidence level, emotions, physical sensations (most notably tension), body language, focus, and thoughts as this occurs.	Notes on your horse's mood, confidence level, emotional state, physical qualities (most notably tension), body language, and focus as this occurs.	Observations on the relationship between these elements, patterns, and the components that contribute to ease and harmony or tension and imbalance.
1.			
2.			
3.			

Notable circumstance.	Notes on your mood, confidence level, emotions, physical sensations (most notably tension), body language, focus, and thoughts as this occurs.	Notes on your horse's mood, confidence level, emotional state, physical qualities (most notably tension), body language, and focus as this occurs.	Observations on the relationship between these elements, patterns, and the components that contribute to ease and harmony or tension and imbalance.
4.			
5.			
6.			

3.   What stands out to you the most about the notable moments you recorded in the chart?

_____

_____

_____

_____

4.   What went well? What would you like to change or do differently?

_____

_____

_____

_____

5.   If there is something you would like to change or do differently what outcome would you like to experience and what are the steps you can take to affect that outcome?

_____

_____

_____

_____

Step 5: "Mane" Event Post-Assessment

*For additional guidance reference Part 2, Step 5

1.   What do you notice now about your breath and that of your horse? Breathe in sync with him again as you did prior to grooming. Describe this experience for you now and reflect on how it compares to the previous time.

_____

_____

_____

_____

2.   Are you finding it easier or more difficult to stay in the moment at this time? What does this tell you about yourself?

_____

_____

_____

_____

3. Describe your present state of being considering your mood, confidence level, emotions, physical sensations, body language, focus, and thoughts. How do these observations compare to your previous observations?

_____

_____

_____

_____

4. Describe your horse's present state of being considering his mood, confidence level, emotional state, physical qualities, body language, and focus. How do these observations compare to your previous observations?

_____

_____

_____

_____

5.	How do you thank your horse for his effort and participation during your time together or as you are saying good bye to him? How does he react to this?

_____

_____

_____

_____

6.	Is there anything you would like to change about this interaction? If so, what steps do you need to take to enact that change?

_____

_____

_____

_____

7.	What stands out to you, or what is your biggest take-away from today?

_____

_____

_____

_____

Step 6: Life applications

*For additional guidance reference Part 2, Step 6

1.   What have you learned or experienced today with your horse that would be helpful in other areas of your life? Describe the circumstance(s) in which what you've learned would be helpful.

_____

_____

_____

_____

2.   What might the result be of applying what you've learned to this other circumstance?

_____

_____

_____

_____

3.   If you had to pick one application, skill, or exercise that you feel would be easiest to start with to integrate into a situation outside of time spent with your horse, what would it be?

_____

_____

_____

_____

4.   Challenge yourself to commit to applying what you've learned here to some situation outside of being with your horse. Describe that experience and the outcome here.

_____

_____

_____

_____

5.   What difference do you notice in yourself after practicing mindfulness in other areas of your life?

_____

_____

_____

_____

6.   What differences do you notice in those around you after practicing mindfulness in other areas of your life? How has the change you've made in yourself rippled out to others connected to you?

_____

_____

_____

_____

Session 2

"Horses are very keen on body language, and what I refer to as "presence", and expression. They know quite a bit about you before you ever get to 'em. They can read things about you clear across an arena."

- Buck Brannaman

Date: _____ Time: _____

Additional notes:

_____

_____

_____

_____

Step 1: Arrival, approach, and greeting

*For additional guidance reference Part 2, Step 1

1.   Upon arrival to where your horse is kept, check in with your breath and 5 senses. How would you describe your breath? What do you see? Hear? Smell? Taste? Feel?

_____

_____

_____

_____

2.   Describe your experience with this first exercise? How is this different from your usual arrival to where your horse lives?

_____

_____

_____

_____

3.   As you approach your horse what do you notice in yourself? Describe any feelings, sensations, or emotions you experience as you approach your horse. Do they change or stay the same? How do you react to them?

_____

_____

_____

_____

4.   How is your horse reacting to you? Describe any communication coming from him in the form of body language, posture, positioning, breathing, and expressions. Does he change or stay the same? How do you react to him?

_____

_____

_____

_____

5. When and how do you greet your horse? When and how does he greet you?

_____

_____

_____

_____

6. How does this differ from the usual way you approach and greet your horse?

_____

_____

_____

_____

Step 2: Grooming and preparing

*For additional guidance reference Part 2, Step 2

1.   What do you notice about your preparation area? Is there anything you would like to have or do differently? If so, what steps can you take to make those changes?

_____

_____

_____

_____

2.   Describe the experience of breathing with your horse. What benefit does this exercise give you? How does your horse react to synchronized breathing?

_____

_____

_____

_____

3.   How often do you repeat the mindfulness exercises of noticing your breath and checking in with your 5 senses? What affect does this have on keeping you present and aware of your environment and horse? What other sensations, feelings, emotions, or thought patterns do you notice while checking in with yourself?

_____

_____

_____

_____

4.   While grooming and preparing your horse, what communication(s) do you receive from him in the form of changes in body language, posture, positioning, breathing, and expressions? What is occurring that causes your horse to express this to you? What might he be communicating to you?

_____

_____

_____

_____

5.   At the time of this communication what do you notice in yourself as far as feelings, sensations, emotions, or thoughts? What would you like to do as a result of this communication?

_____

_____

_____

_____

6.   What, if any, changes would you or your horse like to make in the grooming and preparation process? What steps do you need to take to make those changes? What might be the result of those changes?

_____

_____

_____

_____

Step 3: "Mane" event pre-assessment

*For additional guidance reference Part 2, Step 3

1.   As you make final preparations or adjustments what do you notice about your breath? About your horse's breath? What is registering in each of your 5 senses?

_____

_____

_____

_____

2.   Describe your mood, confidence level, emotions, body language, focus, and thoughts. What effect, if any, are these having on your horse?

_____

_____

_____

_____

3.   Observe your horse. Describe his mood, confidence level, emotional state, and focus. Challenge yourself to base these observations on his body language, expression, and posture to avoid projecting. What effect, if any, are these having on you?

_____

_____

_____

_____

4.   What communications are you getting from your horse as you make final preparations?

_____

_____

_____

_____

5.   Based on your observations of your own and your horse's current states of being, what is the next best step to take?

_____

_____

_____

_____

6.   What, if anything, would you like to be experiencing differently right now? What steps can you take to make your pre-session experience better for you and/or your horse?

_____

_____

_____

_____

Step 4: "Mane" event

*For additional guidance reference Part 2, Step 4

1.   How are you reminding yourself to stay present, notice your breath, and check in with your 5 senses? Describe the effect these reminders are having on your level of presence and ability to stay in the moment. How often do these reminders interrupt unnecessary thoughts, a negative mental tape-loop, or worries about the future?

_____

_____

_____

_____

2.   Use the following chart to track notable circumstances, changes, or events (positive or negative). With each circumstance note your mood, confidence level, emotions, physical sensations (most notably tension), body language, focus, and thoughts. Also note your horse's mood, confidence level, emotional state, physical qualities (most notably tension), body language, and focus. Then record any correlations or patterns you see developing.

Notable circumstance.	Notes on your mood, confidence level, emotions, physical sensations (most notably tension), body language, focus, and thoughts as this occurs.	Notes on your horse's mood, confidence level, emotional state, physical qualities (most notably tension), body language, and focus as this occurs.	Observations on the relationship between these elements, patterns, and the components that contribute to ease and harmony or tension and imbalance.
1.			
2.			
3.			

Notable circumstance.	Notes on your mood, confidence level, emotions, physical sensations (most notably tension), body language, focus, and thoughts as this occurs.	Notes on your horse's mood, confidence level, emotional state, physical qualities (most notably tension), body language, and focus as this occurs.	Observations on the relationship between these elements, patterns, and the components that contribute to ease and harmony or tension and imbalance.
4.			
5.			
6.			

3.   What stands out to you the most about the notable moments you recorded in the chart?

_____

_____

_____

_____

4.   What went well? What would you like to change or do differently?

_____

_____

_____

_____

5.   If there is something you would like to change or do differently what outcome would you like to experience and what are the steps you can take to affect that outcome?

_____

_____

_____

_____

Step 5: "Mane" Event Post-Assessment

*For additional guidance reference Part 2, Step 5

1.   What do you notice now about your breath and that of your horse? Breathe in sync with him again as you did prior to grooming. Describe this experience for you now and reflect on how it compares to the previous time.

_____

_____

_____

_____

2.   Are you finding it easier or more difficult to stay in the moment at this time? What does this tell you about yourself?

_____

_____

_____

_____

3.   Describe your present state of being considering your mood, confidence level, emotions, physical sensations, body language, focus, and thoughts. How do these observations compare to your previous observations?

_____

_____

_____

_____

4.   Describe your horse's present state of being considering his mood, confidence level, emotional state, physical qualities, body language, and focus. How do these observations compare to your previous observations?

_____

_____

_____

_____

5. How do you thank your horse for his effort and participation during your time together or as you are saying goodbye to him? How does he react to this?

_____

_____

_____

_____

6. Is there anything you would like to change about this interaction? If so, what steps do you need to take to enact that change?

_____

_____

_____

_____

7. What stands out to you, or what is your biggest take-away from today?

_____

_____

_____

_____

Step 6: Life applications

*For additional guidance reference Part 2, Step 6

1.   What have you learned or experienced through these exercises that would be helpful in other areas of your life? Describe the circumstance(s) in which what you've learned would be helpful.

_____

_____

_____

_____

2.   What might the result be of applying what you've learned to this other circumstance?

_____

_____

_____

_____

3.   If you had to pick one application, skill, or exercise that you feel would be easiest to start with to integrate into a situation outside of time spent with your horse, what would it be?

_____

_____

_____

_____

4.   Challenge yourself to commit to applying what you've learned here to some situation outside of being with your horse. Describe that experience and the outcome here.

_____

_____

_____

_____

5.   What difference do you notice in yourself after practicing mindfulness in other areas of your life?

_____

_____

_____

_____

6.   What differences do you notice in those around you after practicing mindfulness in other areas of your life? How has the change you've made in yourself rippled out to others connected to you?

_____

_____

_____

_____

<u>Session 3</u>

"MIndfulness is paying attention on purpose, in the present moment, and nonjudgmentally, to the unfolding of experience moment to moment."
-Jon Kabat-Zinn

Date: _____ Time: _____

Additional notes:

_____

_____

_____

_____

Step 1: Arrival, approach, and greeting

*For additional guidance reference Part 2, Step 1

1. Upon arrival to where your horse is kept, check in with your breath and 5 senses. How would you describe your breath? What do you see? Hear? Smell? Taste? Feel?

_____

_____

_____

_____

2. Describe your experience with this first exercise. How is this different from your usual arrival to where your horse lives?

_____

_____

_____

_____

3. As you approach your horse what do you notice in yourself? Describe any feelings, sensations, or emotions you experience as you approach your horse. Do they change or stay the same? How do you react to them?

_____

_____

_____

_____

4. How is your horse reacting to you? Describe any communication coming from him in the form of body language, posture, positioning, breathing, and expressions. Does he change or stay the same? How do you react to him?

_____

_____

_____

_____

5.   When and how do you greet your horse? When and how does he greet you?

_____

_____

_____

_____

6.   How does this differ from the usual way you approach and greet your horse?

_____

_____

_____

_____

Step 2: Grooming and preparing

*For additional guidance reference Part 2, Step 2

1.   What do you notice about your preparation area? Is there anything you would like to have or do differently? If so, what steps can you take to make those changes?

_____

_____

_____

_____

2.   Describe the experience of breathing with your horse. What benefit does this exercise give you? How does your horse react to synchronized breathing?

_____

_____

_____

_____

3.   How often do you repeat the mindfulness exercises of noticing your breath and checking in with your 5 senses? What affect does this have on keeping you present and aware of your environment and horse? What other sensations, feelings, emotions, or thought patterns do you notice while checking in with yourself?

_____

_____

_____

_____

4.   While grooming and preparing your horse, what communication(s) do you receive from him in the form of changes in body language, posture, positioning, breathing, and expressions? What is occurring that causes your horse to express this to you? What might he be communicating to you?

_____

_____

_____

_____

5. At the time of this communication what do you notice in yourself as far as feelings, sensations, emotions, or thoughts? What would you like to do as a result of this communication?

_____

_____

_____

_____

6. What, if any, changes would you or your horse like to make in the grooming and preparation process? What steps do you need to take to make those changes? What might be the result of those changes?

_____

_____

_____

_____

Step 3: "Mane" event pre-assessment

For more guidance reference Part 2, Step 3

1.   As you make final preparations or adjustments what do you notice about your breath? About your horse's breath? What is registering in each of your 5 senses?

_____

_____

_____

_____

2.   Describe your mood, confidence level, emotions, body language, focus, and thoughts. What effect, if any, are these having on your horse?

_____

_____

_____

_____

3. Observe your horse. Describe his mood, confidence level, emotional state, and focus. Challenge yourself to base these observations on his body language, expression, and posture to avoid projecting. What effect, if any, are these having on you?

_____

_____

_____

_____

4. What communications are you getting from your horse as you make your final preparations?

_____

_____

_____

_____

5.   Based on your observations of your own and your horse's current states of being, what is the next best step to take?

_____

_____

_____

_____

6.   What, if anything, would you like to be experiencing differently right now? What steps can you take to make your pre-session experience better for you and/or your horse?

_____

_____

_____

_____

Step 4: "Mane" event

*For additional guidance reference Part 2, Step 4

1.   How are you reminding yourself to stay present, notice your breath, and check in with your 5 senses? Describe the effect these reminders are having on your level of presence and ability to stay in the moment. How often do these reminders interrupt unnecessary thoughts, a negative mental tape-loop, or worries about the future?

_____

_____

_____

_____

2.   Use the following chart to track notable circumstances, changes, or events (positive or negative). With each circumstance note your mood, confidence level, emotions, physical sensations (most notably tension), body language, focus, and thoughts. Also note your horse's mood, confidence level, emotional state, physical qualities (most notably tension), body language, and focus. Then record any correlations or patterns you see developing.

Notable circumstance.	Notes on your mood, confidence level, emotions, physical sensations (most notably tension), body language, focus, and thoughts as this occurs.	Notes on your horse's mood, confidence level, emotional state, physical qualities (most notably tension), body language, and focus as this occurs.	Observations on the relationship between these elements, patterns, and the components that contribute to ease and harmony or tension and imbalance.
1.			
2.			
3.			

Notable circumstance.	Notes on your mood, confidence level, emotions, physical sensations (most notably tension), body language, focus, and thoughts as this occurs.	Notes on your horse's mood, confidence level, emotional state, physical qualities (most notably tension), body language, and focus as this occurs.	Observations on the relationship between these elements, patterns, and the components that contribute to ease and harmony or tension and imbalance.
4.			
5.			
6.			

3.   What stands out to you the most about the notable moments you recorded in the chart?

_____

_____

_____

_____

4.   What went well? What would you like to change or do differently?

_____

_____

_____

_____

5.   If there is something you would like to change or do differently what outcome would you like to experience and what are the steps you can take to affect that outcome?

_____

_____

_____

_____

Step 5: "Mane" Event Post-Assessment

*For additional guidance reference Part 2, Step 5

1.   What do you notice now about your breath and that of your horse? Breathe in sync with him again as you did prior to grooming. Describe this experience for you now and reflect on how it compares to the previous time.

_____

_____

_____

_____

2.   Are you finding it easier or more difficult to stay in the moment at this time? What does this tell you about yourself?

_____

_____

_____

_____

3.   Describe your present state of being considering your mood, confidence level, emotions, physical sensations, body language, focus, and thoughts. How do these observations compare to your previous observations?

_____

_____

_____

_____

4.   Describe your horse's present state of being considering his mood, confidence level, emotional state, physical qualities, body language, and focus. How do these observations compare to your previous observations?

_____

_____

_____

_____

5. How do you thank your horse for his effort and participation during your time together or as you are saying goodbye to him? How does he react to this?

_____

_____

_____

_____

6. Is there anything you would like to change about this interaction? If so, what steps do you need to take to enact that change?

_____

_____

_____

_____

7. What stands out to you, or what is your biggest take-away from today?

_____

_____

_____

_____

Step 6: Life applications

*For additional guidance reference Part 2, Step 6

1.   What have you learned or experienced through these exercises that would be helpful in other areas of your life? Describe the circumstance(s) in which what you've learned would be helpful.

_____

_____

_____

_____

2.   What might the result be of applying what you've learned to this other circumstance?

_____

_____

_____

_____

3.   If you had to pick one application, skill, or exercise that you feel would be easiest to start with to integrate into a situation outside of time spent with your horse, what would it be?

_____

_____

_____

_____

4.   Challenge yourself to commit to applying what you've learned here to some situation outside of being with your horse. Describe that experience and the outcome here.

_____

_____

_____

_____

5.   What difference do you notice in yourself after practicing mindfulness in other areas of your life?

_____

_____

_____

_____

6.   What differences do you notice in those around you after practicing mindfulness in other areas of your life? How has the change you've made in yourself rippled out to others connected to you?

_____

_____

_____

_____

Session 4

"**Between stimulus and response there is a space. In that space is our power to choose our response. In our response lies our growth and our freedom.**"
–*Victor Frankl*

Date: _____ Time: _____

Additional notes:

_____

_____

_____

_____

Step 1: Arrival, approach, and greeting

*For additional guidance reference Part 2, Step 1

1.   Upon arrival to where your horse is kept, check in with your breath and 5 senses. How would you describe your breath? What do you see? Hear? Smell? Taste? Feel?

_____

_____

_____

_____

2.   Describe your experience with this exercise. Now that you have completed several sessions in this journal, how is this exercise changing or evolving for you? How is mindfulness enhancing or enriching this moment for you?

_____

_____

_____

_____

3. As you approach your horse what do you notice in yourself? Describe any feelings, sensations, or emotions you experience as you approach your horse. Do they change or stay the same? How do you react to them?

_____

_____

_____

_____

4. How is your horse reacting to you? Describe any communication coming from him in the form of body language, posture, positioning, breathing, and expressions. Does he change or stay the same? How do you react to him?

_____

_____

_____

_____

5.   When and how do you greet your horse? When and how does he greet you?

_____

_____

_____

_____

6.   What is the most notable aspect of your approach to and greeting of your horse. What does this tell you about yourself? Your horse? Your relationship with him?

_____

_____

_____

_____

Step 2: Grooming and preparing

*For additional guidance reference Part 2, Step 2

1.   If you have experimented with or made any changes to your grooming and preparation area regarding timing, set-up ,location, etc., how have those changes affected this part of your time with your horse?

_____

_____

_____

_____

2.   Describe the experience of breathing with your horse. What benefit does this exercise give you? How does your horse react to synchronized breathing?

_____

_____

_____

_____

3.   How often do you repeat the mindfulness exercises of noticing your breath and checking in with your 5 senses? What affect does this have on keeping you present and aware of your environment and horse? What other sensations, feelings, emotions, or thought patterns do you notice while checking in with yourself?

_____

_____

_____

_____

4.   While grooming and making preparations for the main activity with your horse, what communication(s) do you receive from him in the form of changes in body language, posture, positioning, breathing, and expressions? What is occurring that causes your horse to express this to you? What might he be communicating to you?

_____

_____

_____

_____

5.   At the time of this communication what do you notice in yourself as far as feelings, sensations, emotions, or thoughts? What would you like to do as a result of this communication?

_____

_____

_____

_____

6.   Narrate the preparation process from your horse's perspective. Challenge yourself to base the narration on body language and communications from your horse to avoid projecting.

_____

_____

_____

_____

Step 3: "Mane" event pre-assessment

For more guidance reference Part 2, Step 3

1.   As you make final preparations or adjustments what do you notice about your breath? About your horse's breath? What is registering in each of your 5 senses?

_____

_____

_____

_____

2.   Describe your mood, confidence level, emotions, body language, focus, and thoughts. What effect, if any, are these having on your horse?

_____

_____

_____

_____

3.   Observe your horse. Describe his mood, confidence level, emotional state, and focus. Challenge yourself to base these observations on his body language, expression, and posture to avoid projecting. What effect, if any, are these having on you?

_____

_____

_____

_____

4.   What communications are you getting from your horse as you make final preparations?

_____

_____

_____

_____

5.   Based on your observations of your own and your horse's current states of being, what is the next best step to take?

_____

_____

_____

_____

6.   What, if anything, would you like to be experiencing differently right now? What steps can you take to make your pre-session experience better for you and/or your horse?

_____

_____

_____

_____

Step 4: "Mane" event

*For additional guidance reference Part 2, Step 4

1.   How are you reminding yourself to stay present, notice your breath, and check in with your 5 senses? Describe the effect these reminders are having on your level of presence and ability to stay in the moment. How often do these reminders interrupt unnecessary thoughts, a negative mental tape-loop, or worries about the future?

_____

_____

_____

_____

2.   Use the following chart to track notable circumstances, changes, or events (positive or negative). With each circumstance note your mood, confidence level, emotions, physical sensations (most notably tension), body language, focus, and thoughts. Also note your horse's mood, confidence level, emotional state, physical qualities (most notably tension), body language, and focus. Then record any correlations or patterns you see developing.

Notable circumstance.	Notes on your mood, confidence level, emotions, physical sensations (most notably tension), body language, focus, and thoughts as this occurs.	Notes on your horse's mood, confidence level, emotional state, physical qualities (most notably tension), body language, and focus as this occurs.	Observations on the relationship between these elements, patterns, and the components that contribute to ease and harmony or tension and imbalance.
1.			
2.			
3.			

Notable circumstance.	Notes on your mood, confidence level, emotions, physical sensations (most notably tension), body language, focus, and thoughts as this occurs.	Notes on your horse's mood, confidence level, emotional state, physical qualities (most notably tension), body language, and focus as this occurs.	Observations on the relationship between these elements, patterns, and the components that contribute to ease and harmony or tension and imbalance.
4.			
5.			
6.			

3.   What stands out to you the most about the notable moments you recorded in the chart?

_____

_____

_____

_____

4.   What went well? What would you like to change or do differently?

_____

_____

_____

_____

5.   If there is something you would like to change or do differently what outcome would you like to experience and what are the steps you can take to affect that outcome?

_____

_____

_____

_____

6.   What benefits are mindfulness and increased awareness bringing to you, your horse, and your relationship at this time?

_____

_____

_____

_____

7.   If there was another level of mindfulness to bring to your interactions at this time what would it be? Challenge yourself to explore that and record your experience here.

_____

_____

_____

_____

Step 5: "Mane" Event Post-Assessment

*For additional guidance reference Part 2, Step 5

1.   What do you notice now about your breath and that of your horse? Breathe in sync with him again as you did prior to grooming. Describe this experience for you now and reflect on how it compares to the previous time.

_____

_____

_____

_____

2.   Are you finding it easier or more difficult to stay in the moment at this time? What does this tell you about yourself?

_____

_____

_____

_____

3.   Describe your present state of being considering your mood, confidence level, emotions, physical sensations, body language, focus, and thoughts. How do these observations compare to your previous observations?

_____

_____

_____

_____

4.   Describe your horse's present state of being considering his mood, confidence level, emotional state, physical qualities, body language, and focus. How do these observations compare to your previous observations?

_____

_____

_____

_____

5.   What patterns or correlations are you noticing at this time?

_____

_____

_____

_____

6.   How do you thank your horse for his effort and participation during your time together or as you are saying goodbye to him? How does he react to this?

_____

_____

_____

_____

7.   What stands out to you, or what is your biggest take-away from today?

_____

_____

_____

_____

Step 6: Life applications

*For additional guidance reference Part 2, Step 6

1.   What have you learned or experienced through these exercises that would be helpful in other areas of your life? Describe the circumstance(s) in which what you've learned would be helpful.

_____

_____

_____

_____

2.   What might the result be of applying what you've learned to this other circumstance?

_____

_____

_____

_____

3.   If you had to pick one application, skill, or exercise that you feel would be easiest to start with to integrate into a situation outside of time spent with your horse, what would it be?

_____

_____

_____

_____

4.   Challenge yourself to commit to applying what you've learned here to some situation outside of being with your horse. Describe that experience and the outcome here.

_____

_____

_____

_____

5.   What difference do you notice in yourself after practicing mindfulness in other areas of your life?

_____

_____

_____

_____

6.   What differences do you notice in those around you after practicing mindfulness in other areas of your life? How has the change you've made in yourself rippled out to others connected to you?

_____

_____

_____

_____

Session 5

"Don't be the rider who gallops all night
and never sees the horse
that is beneath him"
~Rumi

Date: _____ Time: _____

Additional notes:

_____

_____

_____

_____

Step 1: Arrival, approach, and greeting

*For additional guidance reference Part 2, Step 1

1.   Upon arrival to where your horse is kept, check in with your breath and 5 senses. How would you describe your breath? What do you see? Hear? Smell? Taste? Feel?

_____

_____

_____

_____

2.   Describe your experience with this exercise. Now that you have completed several sessions in this journal, how is this exercise changing or evolving for you? How is mindfulness enhancing or enriching this moment for you?

_____

_____

_____

_____

3.   As you approach your horse what do you notice in yourself? Describe any feelings, sensations, or emotions you experience as you approach your horse. Do they change or stay the same? How do you react to them?

_____

_____

_____

_____

4.   How is your horse reacting to you? Describe any communication coming from him in the form of body language, posture, positioning, breathing, and expressions. Does he change or stay the same? How do you react to him?

_____

_____

_____

_____

5. When and how do you greet your horse? When and how does he greet you?

_____

_____

_____

_____

6. What is the most notable aspect of your approach to and greeting of your horse. What does this tell you about yourself? Your horse? Your relationship with him?

_____

_____

_____

_____

Step 2: Grooming and preparing

*For additional guidance reference Part 2, Step 2

1.   If you have experimented with or made any changes to your grooming and preparation area regarding timing, set-up ,location, etc., how have those changes affected this part of your time with your horse?

_____

_____

_____

_____

2.   Describe the experience of breathing with your horse. What benefit does this exercise give you? How does your horse react to synchronized breathing?

_____

_____

_____

_____

3.   How often do you repeat the mindfulness exercises of noticing your breath and checking in with your 5 senses? What affect does this have on keeping you present and aware of your environment and horse? What other sensations, feelings, emotions, or thought patterns do you notice while checking in with yourself?

_____

_____

_____

_____

4.   While grooming and tacking your horse, what communication(s) do you receive from him in the form of changes in body language, posture, positioning, breathing, and expressions? What is occurring that causes your horse to express this to you? What might he be communicating to you?

_____

_____

_____

_____

5.   At the time of this communication what do you notice in yourself as far as feelings, sensations, emotions, or thoughts? What would you like to do as a result of this communication?

_____

_____

_____

_____

6.   Narrate the preparation process from your horse's perspective. Challenge yourself to base the narration on body language and communications from your horse to avoid projecting.

_____

_____

_____

_____

Step 3: "Mane" event pre-assessment

For more guidance reference Part 2, Step 3

1.   As you make final preparations or adjustments what do you notice about your breath? About your horse's breath? What is registering in each of your 5 senses?

_____

_____

_____

_____

2.   Describe your mood, confidence level, emotions, body language, focus, and thoughts. What effect, if any, are these having on your horse?

_____

_____

_____

_____

3.   Observe your horse. Describe his mood, confidence level, emotional state, and focus. Challenge yourself to base these observations on his body language, expression, and posture to avoid projecting. What effect, if any, are these having on you?

_____

_____

_____

_____

4.   What communications are you getting from your horse at this time ?

_____

_____

_____

_____

5.   Based on your observations of your own and your horse's current states of being, what is the next best step to take?

_____

_____

_____

_____

6.   What, if anything, would you like to be experiencing differently right now? What steps can you take to make your pre-session experience better for you and/or your horse?

_____

_____

_____

_____

Step 4: "Mane" event

*For additional guidance reference Part 2, Step 4

1. How are you reminding yourself to stay present, notice your breath, and check in with your 5 senses? Describe the effect these reminders are having on your level of presence and ability to stay in the moment. How often do these reminders interrupt unnecessary thoughts, a negative mental tape-loop, or worries about the future?

_____

_____

_____

_____

2.   Use the following chart to track notable circumstances, changes, or events (positive or negative). With each circumstance note your mood, confidence level, emotions, physical sensations (most notably tension), body language, focus, and thoughts. Also note your horse's mood, confidence level, emotional state, physical qualities (most notably tension), body language, and focus. Then record any correlations or patterns you see developing.

Notable circumstance.	Notes on your mood, confidence level, emotions, physical sensations (most notably tension), body language, focus, and thoughts as this occurs.	Notes on your horse's mood, confidence level, emotional state, physical qualities (most notably tension), body language, and focus as this occurs.	Observations on the relationship between these elements, patterns, and the components that contribute to ease and harmony or tension and imbalance.
1.			
2.			
3.			

Notable circumstance.	Notes on your mood, confidence level, emotions, physical sensations (most notably tension), body language, focus, and thoughts as this occurs.	Notes on your horse's mood, confidence level, emotional state, physical qualities (most notably tension), body language, and focus as this occurs.	Observations on the relationship between these elements, patterns, and the components that contribute to ease and harmony or tension and imbalance.
4.			
5.			
6.			

3. What stands out to you the most about the notable moments you recorded in the chart?

_____

_____

_____

_____

4. What went well? What would you like to change or do differently?

_____

_____

_____

_____

5. If there is something you would like to change or do differently what outcome would you like to experience and what are the steps you can take to affect that outcome?

_____

_____

_____

_____

6.   What benefits are mindfulness and increased awareness bringing to you, your horse, and your relationship at this time?

_____

_____

_____

_____

7.   If there was another level of mindfulness to bring to your interactions what would it be? Challenge yourself to explore that and record your experience here.

_____

_____

_____

_____

Step 5: "Mane" Event Post-Assessment

*For additional guidance reference Part 2, Step 5

1.   What do you notice now about your breath and that of your horse? Breathe in sync with him again as you did prior to grooming. Describe this experience for you now and reflect on how it compares to the previous time.

_____

_____

_____

_____

2.   Are you finding it easier or more difficult to stay in the moment at this time? What does this tell you about yourself?

_____

_____

_____

_____

3.   Describe your present state of being considering your mood, confidence level, emotions, physical sensations, body language, focus, and thoughts. How do these observations compare to your previous ones?

_____

_____

_____

_____

4.   Describe your horse's present state of being considering his mood, confidence level, emotional state, physical qualities, body language, and focus. How do these observations compare to your previous ones?

_____

_____

_____

_____

5.   What patterns or correlations are you noticing at this time?

_____

_____

_____

_____

6. How do you thank your horse for his effort and participation during your time together or as you are saying good bye to him? How does he react to this?

_____

_____

_____

_____

7. What stands out to you, or what is your biggest take-away from today?

_____

_____

_____

_____

Step 6: Life applications

*For additional guidance reference Part 2, Step 6

1.   What have you learned or experienced through these exercises that would be helpful in other areas of your life? Describe the circumstance(s) in which what you've learned would be helpful.

_____

_____

_____

_____

2.   What might the result be of applying what you've learned to this other circumstance?

_____

_____

_____

_____

3.   If you had to pick one application, skill, or exercise that you feel would be easiest to start with to integrate into a situation outside of time spent with your horse, what would it be?

_____

_____

_____

_____

4.   Challenge yourself to commit to applying what you've learned here to some situation outside of being with your horse. Describe that experience and the outcome here.

_____

_____

_____

_____

5.   What difference do you notice in yourself after practicing mindfulness in other areas of your life?

_____

_____

_____

_____

6.   What differences do you notice in those around you after practicing mindfulness in other areas of your life? How has the change you've made in yourself rippled out to others connected to you?

_____

_____

_____

_____

Session 6

"**Mindfulness helps us freeze the frame so that we can become aware of our sensations and experiences as they are, without the distorting coloration of socially conditioned responses or habitual reactions.**"
-Henepola Gunaratana

Date: _____ Time: _____

Additional notes:

_____
_____
_____
_____

Step 1: Arrival, approach, and greeting

*For additional guidance reference Part 2, Step 1

1.   Upon arrival to where your horse is kept, check in with your breath and 5 senses. How would you describe your breath? What do you see? Hear? Smell? Taste? Feel?

_____

_____

_____

_____

2.   Describe your experience with this exercise. Now that you have completed several sessions in this journal, how is this exercise changing or evolving for you? How is mindfulness enhancing or enriching this moment for you?

_____

_____

_____

_____

3.   As you approach your horse what do you notice in yourself? Describe any feelings, sensations, or emotions you experience as you approach your horse. Do they change or stay the same? How do you react to them?

_____

_____

_____

_____

4.   How is your horse reacting to you? Describe any communication coming from him in the form of body language, posture, positioning, breathing, and expressions. Does he change or stay the same? How do you react to him?

_____

_____

_____

_____

5.   When and how do you greet your horse? When and how does he greet you?

_____

_____

_____

_____

6.   What is the most notable aspect of your approach to and greeting of your horse. What does this tell you about yourself? Your horse? Your relationship with him?

_____

_____

_____

_____

Step 2: Grooming and preparing

*For additional guidance reference Part 2, Step 2

1.   If you have experimented with or made any changes to your grooming and preparation area regarding timing, set-up ,location, etc., how have those changes affected this part of your time with your horse?

_____

_____

_____

_____

2.   Describe the experience of breathing with your horse. What benefit does this exercise give you? How does your horse react to synchronized breathing?

_____

_____

_____

_____

3. How often do you repeat the mindfulness exercises of noticing your breath and checking in with your 5 senses? What affect does this have on keeping you present and aware of your environment and horse? What other sensations, feelings, emotions, or thought patterns do you notice while checking in with yourself?

_____

_____

_____

_____

4. While grooming and preparing your horse, what communication(s) do you receive from him in the form of changes in body language, posture, positioning, breathing, and expressions? What is occurring that causes your horse to express this to you? What might he be communicating to you?

_____

_____

_____

_____

5.   At the time of this communication what do you notice in yourself as far as feelings, sensations, emotions, or thoughts? What would you like to do as a result of this communication?

_____

_____

_____

_____

6.   Narrate the preparation process from your horse's perspective. Challenge yourself to base the narration on body language and communications from your horse to avoid projecting.

_____

_____

_____

_____

Step 3: "Mane" event pre-assessment

For more guidance reference Part 2, Step 3

1.   As you make final preparations and adjustments what do you notice about your breath? About your horse's breath? What is registering in each of your 5 senses?

_____

_____

_____

_____

2.   Describe your mood, confidence level, emotions, body language, focus, and thoughts. What effect, if any, are these having on your horse?

_____

_____

_____

_____

3. Observe your horse. Describe his mood, confidence level, emotional state, and focus. Challenge yourself to base these observations on his body language, expression, and posture to avoid projecting. What effect, if any, are these having on you?

_____

_____

_____

_____

4. What communications are you getting from your horse as you make final preparations?

_____

_____

_____

_____

5.   Based on your observations of your own and your horse's current states of being, what is the next best step to take?

_____

_____

_____

_____

6.   What, if anything, would you like to be experiencing differently right now? What steps can you take to make your pre-session experience better for you and/or your horse?

_____

_____

_____

_____

Step 4: "Mane" event

*For additional guidance reference Part 2, Step 4

1.   How are you reminding yourself to stay present, notice your breath, and check in with your 5 senses? Describe the effect these reminders are having on your level of presence and ability to stay in the moment. How often do these reminders interrupt unnecessary thoughts, a negative mental tape-loop, or worries about the future?

_____

_____

_____

_____

2.   Use the following chart to track notable circumstances, changes, or events (positive or negative). With each circumstance note your mood, confidence level, emotions, physical sensations (most notably tension), body language, focus, and thoughts. Also note your horse's mood, confidence level, emotional state, physical qualities (most notably tension), body language, and focus. Then record any correlations or patterns you see developing.

Notable circumstance.	Notes on your mood, confidence level, emotions, physical sensations (most notably tension), body language, focus, and thoughts as this occurs.	Notes on your horse's mood, confidence level, emotional state, physical qualities (most notably tension), body language, and focus as this occurs.	Observations on the relationship between these elements, patterns, and the components that contribute to ease and harmony or tension and imbalance.
1.			
2.			
3.			

Notable circumstance.	Notes on your mood, confidence level, emotions, physical sensations (most notably tension), body language, focus, and thoughts as this occurs.	Notes on your horse's mood, confidence level, emotional state, physical qualities (most notably tension), body language, and focus as this occurs.	Observations on the relationship between these elements, patterns, and the components that contribute to ease and harmony or tension and imbalance.
4.			
5.			
6.			

3.   What stands out to you the most about the notable moments you recorded in the chart?

_____

_____

_____

_____

4.   What went well? What would you like to change or do differently?

_____

_____

_____

_____

5.   If there is something you would like to change or do differently what outcome would you like to experience and what are the steps you can take to affect that outcome?

_____

_____

_____

_____

6. What benefits are mindfulness and increased awareness bringing to you, your horse, and your relationship at this time?

_____

_____

_____

_____

7. If there was another level of mindfulness to bring to your interactions what would it be? Challenge yourself to explore that and record your experience here.

_____

_____

_____

_____

Step 5: "Mane" Event Post-Assessment

*For additional guidance reference Part 2, Step 5

1.   What do you notice now about your breath and that of your horse? Breathe in sync with him again as you did prior to grooming. Describe this experience for you now and reflect on how it compares to the previous time.

_____

_____

_____

_____

2.   Are you finding it easier or more difficult to stay in the moment at this time? What does this tell you about yourself?

_____

_____

_____

_____

3.   Describe your present state of being considering your mood, confidence level, emotions, physical sensations, body language, focus, and thoughts. How do these observations compare to your previous ones?

_____

_____

_____

_____

4.   Describe your horse's present state of being considering his mood, confidence level, emotional state, physical qualities, body language, and focus. How do these observations compare to your previous ones?

_____

_____

_____

_____

5.   What patterns or correlations are you noticing at this time?

_____

_____

_____

_____

6.   How do you thank your horse for his effort and participation during your time together or as you are saying goodbye to him? How does he react to this?

_____

_____

_____

_____

7.   What stands out to you, or what is your biggest take-away from today?

_____

_____

_____

_____

Step 6: Life applications

*For additional guidance reference Part 2, Step 6

1.   What have you learned or experienced through these exercises that would be helpful in other areas of your life? Describe the circumstance(s) in which what you've learned would be helpful.

_____

_____

_____

_____

2.   What might the result be of applying what you've learned to this other circumstance?

_____

_____

_____

_____

3.   If you had to pick one application, skill, or exercise that you feel would be easiest to start with to integrate into a situation outside of time spent with your horse, what would it be?

_____

_____

_____

_____

4.   Challenge yourself to commit to applying what you've learned here to some situation outside of being with your horse. Describe that experience and the outcome here.

_____

_____

_____

_____

5.   What difference do you notice in yourself after practicing mindfulness in other areas of your life?

_____

_____

_____

_____

6.   What differences do you notice in those around you after practicing mindfulness in other areas of your life? How has the change you've made in yourself rippled out to others connected to you?

_____

_____

_____

_____

Session 7

"Honesty is the first chapter in the book of wisdom."

-Thomas Jefferson

Date: _____ Time: _____

Additional notes:

_____

_____

_____

_____

Step 1: Arrival, approach, and greeting

*For additional guidance reference Part 2, Step 1

1.   Upon arrival to where your horse is kept, check in with your breath and 5 senses. How would you describe your breath? What do you see? Hear? Smell? Taste? Feel?

_____

_____

_____

_____

2.	Describe your experience with this exercise. Add to this experience a checking in with yourself on a somatic and emotional level. What sensations and feelings do you notice in your body? Where are they located and how would you describe them? What emotions are you feeling?

_____

_____

_____

_____

3.	As you approach your horse what do you notice in yourself? Describe any feelings, sensations, or emotions you experience as you approach your horse. Do they change or stay the same? How do you react to them?

_____

_____

_____

_____

4.   How is your horse reacting to you?As you approach your horse what do you notice in him? Describe any communication coming from him in the form of body language, posture, positioning, breathing, and expressions. Does he change or stay the same? How do you react to him? What feedback is he giving you regarding your approach?

_____

_____

_____

_____

5.   When and how do you greet your horse? When and how does he greet you?

_____

_____

_____

_____

6.   How has the way you approach and greet your horse changed or evolved over the last several sessions? How has mindfulness enhanced or enriched this situation for you and/or your horse?

_____

_____

_____

_____

Step 2: Grooming and preparing

*For additional guidance reference Part 2, Step 2

1.   Describe the benefits you and your horse are enjoying as a result of your mindfulness practices in your preparations.

_____

_____

_____

_____

2.   Describe the experience of breathing with your horse. What benefit does this exercise give you? How does your horse react to synchronized breathing? How do you react on a somatic level (bodily sensations and feelings) to synchronized breathing?

_____

_____

_____

_____

3.   How often do you repeat the mindfulness exercises of noticing your breath and checking in with your 5 senses? What affect does this have on keeping you present and aware of your environment and horse? What other sensations, feelings, emotions, or thought patterns do you notice while checking in with yourself?

_____

_____

_____

_____

4.   While grooming and preparing your horse, what communication(s) do you receive from him in the form of changes in body language, posture, positioning, breathing, and expressions? What is occurring that causes your horse to express this to you? What might he be communicating to you?

_____

_____

_____

_____

5.   At the time of this communication what do you notice in yourself as far as feelings, sensations, emotions, or thoughts? What would you like to do as a result of this communication?

_____

_____

_____

_____

6.   If you could bring a deeper level of mindfulness or awareness to the grooming and tacking process what would that look like? Describe it here along with your experience of exploring that next level.

_____

_____

_____

_____

Step 3: "Mane" event pre-assessment

For more guidance reference Part 2, Step 3

1.   As you make final preparations and adjustments what do you notice about your breath? About your horse's breath? What is registering in each of your 5 senses?

_____

_____

_____

_____

2.   Describe your mood, confidence level, emotions, body language, focus, and thoughts. What effect, if any, are these having on your horse?

_____

_____

_____

_____

3.   Observe your horse. Describe his mood, confidence level, emotional state, and focus. Challenge yourself to base these observations on his body language, expression, and posture to avoid projecting. What effect, if any, are these having on you?

_____

_____

_____

_____

4.   What communications are you getting from your horse as you make final preparations to ride? How do you react to this?

_____

_____

_____

_____

5.   Based on your observations of your own and your horse's current states of being, what is the next best step to take?

_____

_____

_____

_____

6.   How are mindfulness and increased awareness benefiting you in these pre-session moments? How have they benefited your horse? How have they benefited your relationship?

_____

_____

_____

_____

7.   What patterns or correlations are you becoming aware of after several sessions of mindfulness practice? How has your pre-session routine evolved?

_____

_____

_____

_____

Step 4: "Mane" event

*For additional guidance reference Part 2, Step 4

1.   What method are you using to remind yourself to stay present by noticing your breath and checking in with your 5 senses? How has your ability to stay present in the moment evolved over the last several sessions? How does your horse react when you become present?

_____

_____

_____

_____

2.   Use the following chart to track notable circumstances, changes, or events (positive or negative). With each circumstance note your mood, confidence level, emotions, physical sensations (most notably tension), body language, focus, and thoughts. Also note your horse's mood, confidence level, emotional state, physical qualities (most notably tension), body language, and focus. Then record any correlations or patterns you see developing.

Notable circumstance.	Notes on your mood, confidence level, emotions, physical sensations (most notably tension), body language, focus, and thoughts as this occurs.	Notes on your horse's mood, confidence level, emotional state, physical qualities (most notably tension), body language, and focus as this occurs.	Observations on the relationship between these elements, patterns, and the components that contribute to ease and harmony or tension and imbalance.
1.			
2.			
3.			

Notable circumstance.	Notes on your mood, confidence level, emotions, physical sensations (most notably tension), body language, focus, and thoughts as this occurs.	Notes on your horse's mood, confidence level, emotional state, physical qualities (most notably tension), body language, and focus as this occurs.	Observations on the relationship between these elements, patterns, and the components that contribute to ease and harmony or tension and imbalance.
4.			
5.			
6.			

3. What stands out to you the most about the notable moments you recorded in the chart?

_____

_____

_____

_____

4. What went well? What would you like to change or do differently?

_____

_____

_____

_____

5. If there is something you would like to change or do differently what outcome would you like to experience and what are the steps you can take to affect that outcome?

_____

_____

_____

_____

6.   What benefits are mindfulness and increased awareness bringing to you, your horse, and your relationship during your session?

_____

_____

_____

_____

7.   If there was another level of mindfulness to bring to your interactions what would it be? Challenge yourself to explore that and record your experience here.

_____

_____

_____

_____

Step 5: "Mane" Event Post-Assessment

*For additional guidance reference Part 2, Step 5

1. What do you notice now about your breath and that of your horse? Breathe in sync with him again as you did prior to grooming. Describe this experience for you now and reflect on how it compares to the previous time.

_____

_____

_____

_____

2. How are mindfulness and increased awareness benefiting you, your horse, and your relationship at this time?

_____

_____

_____

_____

3.   Describe your present state of being considering your mood, confidence level, emotions, physical sensations, body language, focus, and thoughts. How do these observations compare to your previous observations?

_____

_____

_____

_____

4.   Describe your horse's present state of being considering his mood, confidence level, emotional state, physical qualities, body language, and focus. How do these observations compare to your previous observations?

_____

_____

_____

_____

5.   What patterns or correlations are you noticing at this time?

_____

_____

_____

_____

6.   How do you thank your horse for his effort and participation during your time together or as you are saying good bye to him? How does he react to this? What is he communicating to you at this time?

_____

_____

_____

_____

7.   What stands out to you, or what is your biggest take-away from today?

_____

_____

_____

_____

Step 6: Life applications

*For additional guidance reference Part 2, Step 6

1.   What have you learned or experienced through these exercises that would be helpful in other areas of your life? Describe the circumstance(s) in which what you've learned would be helpful.

_____

_____

_____

_____

2.   What might the result be of applying what you've learned to this other circumstance?

_____

_____

_____

_____

3. If you had to pick one application, skill, or exercise that you feel would be easiest to start with to integrate into a situation outside of time spent with your horse, what would it be?

_____

_____

_____

_____

4. Challenge yourself to commit to applying what you've learned here to some situation outside of being with your horse. Describe that experience and the outcome here.

_____

_____

_____

_____

5.   What difference do you notice in yourself after practicing mindfulness in other areas of your life?

_____

_____

_____

_____

6.   What differences do you notice in those around you after practicing mindfulness in other areas of your life? How has the change you've made in yourself rippled out to others connected to you?

_____

_____

_____

_____

Session 8

"I accept relationship as my primary teacher about myself, other people, and the mysteries of the universe."
- *Gay Hendricks*

Date: _____ Time: _____

Additional notes:

_____

_____

_____

_____

Step 1: Arrival, approach, and greeting

*For additional guidance reference Part 2, Step 1

1.   Upon arrival to where your horse is kept, check in with your breath and 5 senses. How would you describe your breath? What do you see? Hear? Smell? Taste? Feel?

_____

_____

_____

_____

2. Describe your experience with this exercise. Add to this experience a checking in with yourself on a somatic and emotional level. What sensations and feelings do you notice in your body? Where are they located and how would you describe them? What emotions are you feeling?

_____

_____

_____

_____

3. As you approach your horse what do you notice in yourself? Describe any feelings, sensations, or emotions you experience as you approach your horse. Do they change or stay the same? How do you react to them?

_____

_____

_____

_____

4.   How is your horse reacting to you? As you approach your horse what do you notice in him? Describe any communication coming from him in the form of body language, posture, positioning, breathing, and expressions. Does he change or stay the same? How do you react to him? What feedback is he giving you regarding your approach?

_____

_____

_____

_____

5.   When and how do you greet your horse? When and how does he greet you?

_____

_____

_____

_____

6.   How has the way you approach and greet your horse changed or evolved over the last several sessions? How has mindfulness enhanced or enriched this situation for you and/or your horse?

_____

_____

_____

_____

Step 2: Grooming and preparing

*For additional guidance reference Part 2, Step 2

1.   Describe the benefits you and your horse are enjoying as a result of your mindfulness practices in your preparations.

_____

_____

_____

_____

2.   Describe the experience of breathing with your horse. What benefit does this exercise give you? How does your horse react to synchronized breathing? How do you react on a somatic level (bodily sensations and feelings) to synchronized breathing?

_____

_____

_____

_____

3.   How often do you repeat the mindfulness exercises of noticing your breath and checking in with your 5 senses? What affect does this have on keeping you present and aware of your environment and horse? What other sensations, feelings, emotions, or thought patterns do you notice while checking in with yourself?

_____

_____

_____

_____

4.   While grooming and preparing your horse, what communication(s) do you receive from him in the form of changes in body language, posture, positioning, breathing, and expressions? What is occurring that causes your horse to express this to you? What might he be communicating to you?

_____

_____

_____

_____

5.   At the time of this communication what do you notice in yourself as far as feelings, sensations, emotions, or thoughts? What would you like to do as a result of this communication?

_____

_____

_____

_____

6.   If you could bring a deeper level of mindfulness or awareness to the grooming and tacking process what would that look like? Describe it here along with your experience of exploring that next level.

_____

_____

_____

_____

Step 3: "Mane" event pre-assessment

For more guidance reference Part 2, Step 3

1.   As you make final preparations and adjustments what do you notice about your breath? About your horse's breath? What is registering in each of your 5 senses?

_____

_____

_____

_____

2.   Describe your mood, confidence level, emotions, body language, focus, and thoughts. What effect, if any, are these having on your horse?

_____

_____

_____

_____

3.   Observe your horse. Describe his mood, confidence level, emotional state, and focus. Challenge yourself to base these observations on his body language, expression, and posture to avoid projecting. What effect, if any, are these having on you?

_____

_____

_____

_____

4.   What communications are you getting from your horse as you make final preparations? How do you react to this?

_____

_____

_____

_____

5. Based on your observations of your own and your horse's current states of being, what is the next best step to take?

_____

_____

_____

_____

6. How have mindfulness and increased awareness benefited you in these pre-ride moments? How have they benefited your horse? How have they benefited your relationship?

_____

_____

_____

_____

7. What patterns or correlations are you becoming aware of after several sessions of pre-ride mindfulness practice? How has your pre-ride routine evolved?

_____

_____

_____

_____

Step 4: "Mane" event

*For additional guidance reference Part 2, Step 4

1.   What method are you using to remind yourself to stay present by noticing your breath and checking in with your 5 senses? How has your ability to stay present in the moment evolved over the last several sessions? How does your horse react when you become present?

_____

_____

_____

_____

2.   Use the following chart to track notable circumstances, changes, or events (positive or negative). With each circumstance note your mood, confidence level, emotions, physical sensations (most notably tension), body language, focus, and thoughts. Also note your horse's mood, confidence level, emotional state, physical qualities (most notably tension), body language, and focus. Then record any correlations or patterns you see developing.

Notable circumstance.	Notes on your mood, confidence level, emotions, physical sensations (most notably tension), body language, focus, and thoughts as this occurs.	Notes on your horse's mood, confidence level, emotional state, physical qualities (most notably tension), body language, and focus as this occurs.	Observations on the relationship between these elements, patterns, and the components that contribute to ease and harmony or tension and imbalance.
1.			
2.			
3.			

Notable circumstance.	Notes on your mood, confidence level, emotions, physical sensations (most notably tension), body language, focus, and thoughts as this occurs.	Notes on your horse's mood, confidence level, emotional state, physical qualities (most notably tension), body language, and focus as this occurs.	Observations on the relationship between these elements, patterns, and the components that contribute to ease and harmony or tension and imbalance.
4.			
5.			
6.			

3.   What stands out to you the most about the notable moments you recorded in the chart?

_____

_____

_____

_____

4.   What went well? What would you like to change or do differently?

_____

_____

_____

_____

5.   If there is something you would like to change or do differently what outcome would you like to experience and what are the steps you can take to affect that outcome?

_____

_____

_____

_____

6. What benefits are mindfulness and increased awareness bringing to you, your horse, and your relationship during your session?

_____

_____

_____

_____

7. If there was another level of mindfulness to bring to your interactions what would it be? Challenge yourself to explore that and record your experience here.

_____

_____

_____

_____

Step 5: "Mane" Event Post-Assessment

*For additional guidance reference Part 2, Step 5

1.   What do you notice now about your breath and that of your horse? Breathe in sync with him again as you did prior to grooming. Describe this experience for you now and reflect on how it compares to the previous time.

_____

_____

_____

_____

2.   How are mindfulness and increased awareness benefiting you, your horse, and your relationship at this time?

_____

_____

_____

_____

3.   Describe your present state of being considering your mood, confidence level, emotions, physical sensations, body language, focus, and thoughts. How do these observations compare to your previous observations?

_____

_____

_____

_____

4.   Describe your horse's present state of being considering his mood, confidence level, emotional state, physical qualities, body language, and focus. How do these observations compare to your previous observations?

_____

_____

_____

_____

5.   What patterns or correlations are you noticing at this time?

_____

_____

_____

_____

6.   How do you thank your horse for his effort and participation during your time together or as you are saying good bye to him? How does he react to this? What is he communicating to you at this time?

_____

_____

_____

_____

7.   What stands out to you, or what is your biggest take-away from today?

_____

_____

_____

_____

Step 6: Life applications

*For additional guidance reference Part 2, Step 6

1.   What have you learned or experienced through these exercises that would be helpful in other areas of your life? Describe the circumstance(s) in which what you've learned would be helpful.

_____

_____

_____

_____

2.   What might the result be of applying what you've learned to this other circumstance?

_____

_____

_____

_____

3. If you had to pick one application, skill, or exercise that you feel would be easiest to start with to integrate into a situation outside of time spent with your horse, what would it be?

_____

_____

_____

_____

4. Challenge yourself to commit to applying what you've learned here to some situation outside of being with your horse. Describe that experience and the outcome here.

_____

_____

_____

_____

5.   What difference do you notice in yourself after practicing mindfulness in other areas of your life?

_____

_____

_____

_____

6.   What differences do you notice in those around you after practicing mindfulness in other areas of your life? How has the change you've made in yourself rippled out to others connected to you?

_____

_____

_____

_____

Session 9

"I'm interested in learning that's motivated by reverence for life, that's motivated by a desire to learn skills, to learn new things that help us to better contribute to our own well-being and the well-being of others. And what fills me with great sadness is any learning that I see motivated by coercion."
- Marshall Rosenberg

Date: _____ Time: _____

Additional notes:

_____
_____
_____
_____

Step 1: Arrival, approach, and greeting

*For additional guidance reference Part 2, Step 1

1.   Upon arrival to where your horse is kept, check in with your breath and 5 senses. How would you describe your breath? What do you see? Hear? Smell? Taste? Feel?

_____

_____

_____

_____

2.   Describe your experience with this exercise. Add to this experience a checking in with yourself on a somatic and emotional level. What sensations and feelings do you notice in your body? Where are they located and how would you describe them? What emotions are you feeling?

_____

_____

_____

_____

3.   As you approach your horse what do you notice in yourself? Describe any feelings, sensations, or emotions you experience as you approach your horse. Do they change or stay the same? How do you react to them?

_____

_____

_____

_____

4. How is your horse reacting to you?As you approach your horse what do you notice in him? Describe any communication coming from him in the form of body language, posture, positioning, breathing, and expressions. Does he change or stay the same? How do you react to him? What feedback is he giving you regarding your approach?

_____
_____
_____
_____

5. When and how do you greet your horse? When and how does he greet you?

_____
_____
_____
_____

6.   How has the way you approach and greet your horse changed or evolved over the last several sessions? How has mindfulness enhanced or enriched this situation for you and/or your horse?

_____

_____

_____

_____

Step 2: Grooming and preparing

*For additional guidance reference Part 2, Step 2

1.   Describe the benefits you and your horse are enjoying as a result of your mindfulness practices in your preparations.

_____

_____

_____

_____

2.   Describe the experience of breathing with your horse. What benefit does this exercise give you? How does your horse react to synchronized breathing? How do you react on a somatic level (bodily sensations and feelings) to synchronized breathing?

_____

_____

_____

_____

3.   How often do you repeat the mindfulness exercises of noticing your breath and checking in with your 5 senses? What affect does this have on keeping you present and aware of your environment and horse? What other sensations, feelings, emotions, or thought patterns do you notice while checking in with yourself?

_____

_____

_____

_____

4.   While grooming and preparing your horse, what communication(s) do you receive from him in the form of changes in body language, posture, positioning, breathing, and expressions? What is occurring that causes your horse to express this to you? What might he be communicating to you?

_____

_____

_____

_____

5.　At the time of this communication what do you notice in yourself as far as feelings, sensations, emotions, or thoughts? What would you like to do as a result of this communication?

_____

_____

_____

_____

6.　If you could bring a deeper level of mindfulness or awareness to your preparation process what would that look like? Describe it here along with your experience of exploring that next level.

_____

_____

_____

_____

Step 3: "Mane" event pre-assessment

For more guidance reference Part 2, Step 3

1.   As you make final preparations and adjustments what do you notice about your breath? About your horse's breath? What is registering in each of your 5 senses?

_____

_____

_____

_____

2.   Describe your mood, confidence level, emotions, body language, focus, and thoughts. What effect, if any, are these having on your horse?

_____

_____

_____

_____

3.   Observe your horse. Describe his mood, confidence level, emotional state, and focus. Challenge yourself to base these observations on his body language, expression, and posture to avoid projecting. What effect, if any, are these having on you?

_____

_____

_____

_____

4.   What communications are you getting from your horse as you make final preparations? How do you react to this?

_____

_____

_____

_____

5.   Based on your observations of your own and your horse's current states of being, what is the next best step to take?

_____

_____

_____

_____

6.   How have mindfulness and increased awareness benefited you in these pre-session moments? How have they benefited your horse? How have they benefited your relationship?

_____

_____

_____

_____

7.   What patterns or correlations are you becoming aware of after several sessions of pre-ride mindfulness practice? How has your pre-ride routine evolved?

_____

_____

_____

_____

Step 4: "Mane" event

*For additional guidance reference Part 2, Step 4

1.   What method are you using to remind yourself to stay present by noticing your breath and checking in with your 5 senses? How has your ability to stay present in the moment evolved over the last several sessions? How does your horse react when you become present?

_____

_____

_____

_____

2.   Use the following chart to track notable circumstances, changes, or events (positive or negative). With each circumstance note your mood, confidence level, emotions, physical sensations (most notably tension), body language, focus, and thoughts. Also note your horse's mood, confidence level, emotional state, physical qualities (most notably tension), body language, and focus. Then record any correlations or patterns you see developing.

Notable circumstance.	Notes on your mood, confidence level, emotions, physical sensations (most notably tension), body language, focus, and thoughts as this occurs.	Notes on your horse's mood, confidence level, emotional state, physical qualities (most notably tension), body language, and focus as this occurs.	Observations on the relationship between these elements, patterns, and the components that contribute to ease and harmony or tension and imbalance.
1.			
2.			
3.			

Notable circumstance.	Notes on your mood, confidence level, emotions, physical sensations (most notably tension), body language, focus, and thoughts as this occurs.	Notes on your horse's mood, confidence level, emotional state, physical qualities (most notably tension), body language, and focus as this occurs.	Observations on the relationship between these elements, patterns, and the components that contribute to ease and harmony or tension and imbalance.
4.			
5.			
6.			

3.   What stands out to you the most about the notable moments you recorded in the chart?

_____

_____

_____

_____

4.   What went well? What would you like to change or do differently?

_____

_____

_____

_____

5.   If there is something you would like to change or do differently what outcome would you like to experience and what are the steps you can take to affect that outcome?

_____

_____

_____

_____

6. What benefits are mindfulness and increased awareness bringing to you, your horse, and your relationship while riding?

_____

_____

_____

_____

7. If there was another level of mindfulness to bring to your riding what would it be? Challenge yourself to explore that and record your experience here.

_____

_____

_____

_____

Step 5: "Mane" Event
Post-Assessment

*For additional guidance reference Part 2, Step 5

1.   What do you notice now about your breath and that of your horse? Breathe in sync with him again as you did prior to grooming. Describe this experience for you now and reflect on how it compares to the previous time.

_____

_____

_____

_____

2.   How are mindfulness and increased awareness benefiting you, your horse, and your relationship at this time?

_____

_____

_____

_____

3.   Describe your present state of being considering your mood, confidence level, emotions, physical sensations, body language, focus, and thoughts. How do these observations compare to your previous observations?

_____

_____

_____

_____

4.   Describe your horse's present state of being considering his mood, confidence level, emotional state, physical qualities, body language, and focus. How do these observations compare to your previous observations?

_____

_____

_____

_____

5.   What patterns or correlations are you noticing at this time?

_____

_____

_____

_____

6.   How do you thank your horse for his effort and participation during your time together or as you are saying good bye to him? How does he react to this? What is he communicating to you at this time?

_____

_____

_____

_____

7.   What stands out to you, or what is your biggest take-away from today?

_____

_____

_____

_____

Step 6: Life applications

*For additional guidance reference Part 2, Step 6

1.   What have you learned or experienced through these exercises that would be helpful in other areas of your life? Describe the circumstance(s) in which what you've learned would be helpful.

_____

_____

_____

_____

2.   What might the result be of applying what you've learned to this other circumstance?

_____

_____

_____

_____

3.   If you had to pick one application, skill, or exercise that you feel would be easiest to start with to integrate into a situation outside of time spent with your horse, what would it be?

_____

_____

_____

_____

4.   Challenge yourself to commit to applying what you've learned here to some situation outside of being with your horse. Describe that experience and the outcome here.

_____

_____

_____

_____

5. What difference do you notice in yourself after practicing mindfulness in other areas of your life?

_____

_____

_____

_____

6. What differences do you notice in those around you after practicing mindfulness in other areas of your life? How has the change you've made in yourself rippled out to others connected to you?

_____

_____

_____

_____

Session 10

"You've always had the power right there in your shoes, you just had to learn it for yourself."
- L. Frank Baum

Date: _____ Time: _____

Additional notes:

_____

_____

_____

_____

Step 1: Arrival, approach, and greeting

*For additional guidance reference Part 2, Step 1

1.   Upon arrival check in with your breath and 5 senses. How would you describe your breath? What do you see? Hear? Smell? Taste? Feel? Check in with yourself on an somatic and emotional level. What sensations and feelings do you notice in your body? Where are they located and how would you describe them? What emotions are you feeling?

_____

_____

_____

_____

2.   What correlations do you notice between these elements? Allow yourself some extra time to explore and track your breath, as well as your sensory and somatic observations. Record your experience here.

_____

_____

_____

_____

3.   As you approach your horse what do you notice in yourself? Describe any feelings, sensations, or emotions you experience as you approach your horse. Do they change or stay the same? How do you react to them?

_____

_____

_____

_____

4.   How is your horse reacting to you? As you approach your horse what do you notice in him? Does he change or stay the same? How do you react to him? What feedback is he giving you regarding your approach?

_____

_____

_____

_____

5.   When and how do you greet your horse? When and how does he greet you? How has this changed over the last several sessions?

_____

_____

_____

_____

6. If there was another level of mindfulness or awareness that you could bring to the approach and greeting of your horse what would it be?

_____

_____

_____

_____

7. Challenge yourself to engage in that next level and record your experience here.

_____

_____

_____

_____

Step 2: Grooming and preparing

*For additional guidance reference Part 2, Step 2

1.   Does your preparation and location for this step remain the same every session or does it vary? Why or why not?

_____

_____

_____

_____

2.   Take a moment to breathe in synchrony with your horse and then continue that exercise, at intervals if necessary, into grooming and tacking. Describe this experience here. How is it different? Does it benefit you? Your horse? If so, how?

_____

_____

_____

_____

3.   How often do you repeat the mindfulness exercises of noticing your breath and checking in with your 5 senses? What affect does this have on keeping you present and aware of your environment and horse? What other sensations, feelings, emotions, or thought patterns do you notice while checking in with yourself?

_____

_____

_____

_____

4.   While grooming and preparing your horse, what communication(s) do you receive from him in the form of changes in body language, posture, positioning, breathing, and expressions? What is occurring that causes your horse to express this to you? What might he be communicating to you?

_____

_____

_____

_____

5. At the time of this communication what do you notice in yourself as far as feelings, sensations, emotions, or thoughts? What would you like to do as a result of this communication?

_____

_____

_____

_____

6. What is your biggest take-away from today's grooming and tacking session?

_____

_____

_____

_____

Step 3: "Mane" event pre-assessment

For more guidance reference Part 2, Step 3

1.   As you make final preparations and adjustments what do you notice about your breath? About your horse's breath? What is registering in each of your 5 senses?

_____

_____

_____

_____

2.   Describe your mood, confidence level, emotions, body language, focus, and thoughts. What effect, if any, are these having on your horse?

_____

_____

_____

_____

3.   Observe your horse. Describe his mood, confidence level, emotional state, and focus. Challenge yourself to base these observations on his body language, expression, and posture to avoid projecting. What effect, if any, are these having on you?

_____

_____

_____

_____

4.   What communications are you getting from your horse as you make final preparations? How do you react to this?

_____

_____

_____

_____

5. Based on your observations of your own and your horse's current states of being, what is the next best step to take?

_____

_____

_____

_____

6. What patterns or correlations are you becoming aware of after several sessions of pre-ride mindfulness practice? How has your pre-session routine evolved?

_____

_____

_____

_____

7. What stands out to you the most at this time? What does that tell you about yourself, your horse, or your relationship?

_____

_____

_____

_____

Step 4: "Mane" event

*For additional guidance reference Part 2, Step 4

1.   What method are you using to remind yourself to stay present by noticing your breath and checking in with your 5 senses? How has your ability to stay present in the moment evolved over the last several sessions? How does your horse react when you become present?

_____

_____

_____

_____

2.   Use the following chart to track notable circumstances, changes, or events (positive or negative). With each circumstance note your mood, confidence level, emotions, physical sensations (most notably tension), body language, focus, and thoughts. Also note your horse's mood, confidence level, emotional state, physical qualities (most notably tension), body language, and focus. Then record any correlations or patterns you see developing.

Notable circumstance.	Notes on your mood, confidence level, emotions, physical sensations (most notably tension), body language, focus, and thoughts as this occurs.	Notes on your horse's mood, confidence level, emotional state, physical qualities (most notably tension), body language, and focus as this occurs.	Observations on the relationship between these elements, patterns, and the components that contribute to ease and harmony or tension and imbalance.
1.			
2.			
3.			

Notable circumstance.	Notes on your mood, confidence level, emotions, physical sensations (most notably tension), body language, focus, and thoughts as this occurs.	Notes on your horse's mood, confidence level, emotional state, physical qualities (most notably tension), body language, and focus as this occurs.	Observations on the relationship between these elements, patterns, and the components that contribute to ease and harmony or tension and imbalance.
4.			
5.			
6.			

3.   What stands out to you the most about the notable moments you recorded in the chart?

_____

_____

_____

_____

4.   What went well? What would you like to change or do differently?

_____

_____

_____

_____

5.   If there is something you would like to change or do differently what outcome would you like to experience and what are the steps you can take to affect that outcome?

_____

_____

_____

_____

6. What benefits are mindfulness and increased awareness bringing to you, your horse, and your relationship at this time?

_____

_____

_____

_____

7. If there was another level of mindfulness to bring to your interactions what would it be? Challenge yourself to explore that and record your experience here.

_____

_____

_____

_____

_____

8. What is your biggest take-away from your session today?

_____

_____

_____

_____

Step 5: "Mane" Event Post-Assessment

*For additional guidance reference Part 2, Step 5

1.   Describe your present state of being considering your mood, confidence level, emotions, physical sensations, body language, focus, and thoughts. How do these observations compare to your previous ones?

_____

_____

_____

_____

2.   Describe your horse's present state of being considering his mood, confidence level, emotional state, physical qualities, body language, and focus. How do these observations compare to your previous ones?

_____

_____

_____

_____

3.   What patterns or correlations are you noticing at this time?

_____

_____

_____

_____

4.   Breathe in synchrony with your horse. Allow yourself some extra time to explore and track your breath, as well as your sensory and somatic observations. Do they change or stay the same? How do you react to this? How does your horse react? Record your experience here.

_____

_____

_____

_____

5.   How do you thank your horse for his effort and participation during your time together or as you are saying good bye to him? How does he react to this? What is he communicating to you at this time?

_____

_____

_____

_____

6.   What stands out to you, or what is your biggest take-away from today?

_____

_____

_____

_____

Step 6: Life applications

*For additional guidance reference Part 2, Step 6

1.   What have you learned or experienced through these exercises that would be helpful in other areas of your life? Describe the circumstance(s) in which what you've learned would be helpful.

_____

_____

_____

_____

2.   What might the result be of applying what you've learned to this other circumstance?

_____

_____

_____

_____

3.   If you had to pick one application, skill, or exercise that you feel would be easiest to start with to integrate into a situation outside of time spent with your horse, what would it be?

_____

_____

_____

_____

4.   Challenge yourself to commit to applying what you've learned here to some situation outside of being with your horse. Describe that experience and the outcome here.

_____

_____

_____

_____

5.   What difference do you notice in yourself after practicing mindfulness in other areas of your life?

_____

_____

_____

_____

6.   What differences do you notice in those around you after practicing mindfulness in other areas of your life? How has the change you've made in yourself rippled out to others connected to you?

_____

_____

_____

_____

Session 11

"**Most of the shadows of life are caused by standing in our own sunshine.**"
-*Ralph Waldo Emerson*

Date: _____ Time: _____

Additional notes:

_____

_____

_____

_____

Step 1: Arrival, approach, and greeting

*For additional guidance reference Part 2, Step 1

1.   Upon arrival check in with your breath and 5 senses. How would you describe your breath? What do you see? Hear? Smell? Taste? Feel? Check in with yourself on an somatic and emotional level. What sensations and feelings do you notice in your body? Where are they located and how would you describe them? What emotions are you feeling?

_____

_____

_____

_____

2. What correlations do you notice between these elements? Allow yourself some extra time to explore and track your breath, as well as your sensory and somatic observations. Record your experience here.

_____

_____

_____

_____

3. As you approach your horse what do you notice in yourself? Describe any feelings, sensations, or emotions you experience as you approach your horse. Do they change or stay the same? How do you react to them?

_____

_____

_____

4. How is your horse reacting to you?As you approach your horse what do you notice in him? Describe any communication coming from him in the form of body language, posture, positioning, breathing, and expressions. Does he change or stay the same? How do you react to him?

_____

_____

_____

_____

5. When and how do you greet your horse? When and how does he greet you? How has this changed over the last several sessions?

_____

_____

_____

_____

6.   If there was another level of mindfulness or awareness that you could bring to the approach and greeting of your horse what would it be?

_____

_____

_____

_____

7.   Challenge yourself to engage in that next level and record your experience here.

_____

_____

_____

_____

Step 2: Grooming and preparing

*For additional guidance reference Part 2, Step 2

1.   Does your preparation and location for this step remain the same every session or does it vary? Why or why not?

_____

_____

_____

_____

2.   Take a moment to breathe in synchrony with your horse and then continue that exercise, at intervals if necessary, into grooming and tacking. Describe this experience here. How is it different? Does it benefit you? Your horse? If so, how?

_____

_____

_____

_____

3. How often do you repeat the mindfulness exercises of noticing your breath and checking in with your 5 senses? What affect does this have on keeping you present and aware of your environment and horse? What other sensations, feelings, emotions, or thought patterns do you notice while checking in with yourself?

_____

_____

_____

_____

4. While grooming and preparing your horse, what communication(s) do you receive from him in the form of changes in body language, posture, positioning, breathing, and expressions? What is occurring that causes your horse to express this to you? What might he be communicating to you?

_____

_____

_____

_____

5.   At the time of this communication what do you notice in yourself as far as feelings, sensations, emotions, or thoughts? What would you like to do as a result of this communication?

_____

_____

_____

_____

6.   What is your biggest take-away from today's grooming and preparation session?

_____

_____

_____

_____

Step 3: "Mane" event pre-assessment

For more guidance reference Part 2, Step 3

1.   As you make final preparations and adjustments what do you notice about your breath? About your horse's breath? What is registering in each of your 5 senses?

_____

_____

_____

_____

2.   What communications are you getting from your horse as you make final preparations?

_____

_____

_____

_____

3.   Describe your mood, confidence level, emotions, body language, focus, and thoughts. What effect, if any, are these having on your horse?

_____

_____

_____

_____

4.   Observe your horse. Describe his mood, confidence level, emotional state, and focus. Challenge yourself to base these observations on his body language, expression, and posture to avoid projecting.

_____

_____

_____

_____

5.   Based on your observations of your own and your horse's current states of being, what is the next best step to take?

_____

_____

_____

_____

6.   What patterns or correlations are you becoming aware of after several sessions of mindfulness practice? How has your pre-session routine evolved?

_____

_____

_____

_____

7.   What stands out to you the most at this time? What does that tell you about yourself, your horse, or your relationship?

_____

_____

_____

_____

Step 4: "Mane" event

*For additional guidance reference Part 2, Step 4

1.　What method are you using to remind yourself to stay present by noticing your breath and checking in with your 5 senses? How has your ability to stay present in the moment evolved over the last several sessions? How does your horse react when you become present?

_____

_____

_____

_____

2.　Use the following chart to track notable circumstances, changes, or events (positive or negative). With each circumstance note your mood, confidence level, emotions, physical sensations (most notably tension), body language, focus, and thoughts. Also note your horse's mood, confidence level, emotional state, physical qualities (most notably tension), body language, and focus. Then record any correlations or patterns you see developing.

Notable circumstance.	Notes on your mood, confidence level, emotions, physical sensations (most notably tension), body language, focus, and thoughts as this occurs.	Notes on your horse's mood, confidence level, emotional state, physical qualities (most notably tension), body language, and focus as this occurs.	Observations on the relationship between these elements, patterns, and the components that contribute to ease and harmony or tension and imbalance.
1.			
2.			
3.			

Notable circumstance.	Notes on your mood, confidence level, emotions, physical sensations (most notably tension), body language, focus, and thoughts as this occurs.	Notes on your horse's mood, confidence level, emotional state, physical qualities (most notably tension), body language, and focus as this occurs.	Observations on the relationship between these elements, patterns, and the components that contribute to ease and harmony or tension and imbalance.
4.			
5.			
6.			

3.   What stands out to you the most about the notable moments you recorded in the chart?

_____

_____

_____

_____

4.   What went well? What would you like to change or do differently?

_____

_____

_____

_____

5.   If there is something you would like to change or do differently what outcome would you like to experience and what are the steps you can take to affect that outcome?

_____

_____

_____

_____

6. What benefits are mindfulness and increased awareness bringing to you, your horse, and your relationship at this time?

_____

_____

_____

_____

7. If there was another level of mindfulness to bring to your interactions what would it be? Challenge yourself to explore that and record your experience here

.

_____

_____

_____

_____

8. What is your biggest take-away from your session today?

_____

_____

_____

_____

Step 5: "Mane" Event Post-Assessment

*For additional guidance reference Part 2, Step 5

1.   Describe your present state of being considering your mood, confidence level, emotions, physical sensations, body language, focus, and thoughts. How do these observations compare to your previous ones?

_____

_____

_____

_____

2.   Describe your horse's present state of being considering his mood, confidence level, emotional state, physical qualities, body language, and focus. How do these observations compare to your previous ones?

_____

_____

_____

_____

3.   What patterns or correlations are you noticing at this time?

_____

_____

_____

_____

4.   Breathe in synchrony with your horse. Allow yourself some extra time to explore and track your breath, as well as your sensory and somatic observations. Record your experience here.
Do they change or stay the same? How do you react to this? How does your horse react?

_____

_____

_____

_____

5.   How do you thank your horse for his effort and participation during your time together or as you are saying good bye to him? How does he react to this? What is he communicating to you at this time?

_____

_____

_____

_____

6.   What stands out to you, or what is your biggest take-away from today?

_____

_____

_____

_____

Step 6: Life applications

*For additional guidance reference Part 2, Step 6

1.   What have you learned or experienced through these exercises that would be helpful in other areas of your life? Describe the circumstance(s) in which what you've learned would be helpful.

_____

_____

_____

_____

2.   What might the result be of applying what you've learned to this other circumstance?

_____

_____

_____

_____

3.　　If you had to pick one application, skill, or exercise that you feel would be easiest to start with to integrate into a situation outside of time spent with your horse, what would it be?

_____

_____

_____

_____

4.　　Challenge yourself to commit to applying what you've learned here to some situation outside of being with your horse. Describe that experience and the outcome here.

.

_____

_____

_____

_____

5. What difference do you notice in yourself after practicing mindfulness in other areas of your life?

_____

_____

_____

_____

6. What differences do you notice in those around you after practicing mindfulness in other areas of your life? How has the change you've made in yourself rippled out to others connected to you?

_____

_____

_____

_____

Session 12

"Be where you are; otherwise you will miss your life."
- *Buddha*

Date: _____ Time: _____

Additional notes:

_____

_____

_____

_____

Step 1: Arrival, approach, and greeting

*For additional guidance reference Part 2, Step 1

1.   Upon arrival check in with your breath and 5 senses. How would you describe your breath? What do you see? Hear? Smell? Taste? Feel? Check in with yourself on an somatic and emotional level. What sensations and feelings do you notice in your body? Where are they located and how would you describe them? What emotions are you feeling?

_____

_____

_____

_____

2.   What correlations do you notice between these elements? Allow yourself some extra time to explore and track your breath, as well as your sensory and somatic observations. Record your experience here.

_____

_____

_____

_____

3.   As you approach your horse what do you notice in yourself? Describe any feelings, sensations, or emotions you experience as you approach your horse. Do they change or stay the same? How do you react to them?

_____

_____

_____

_____

4.   How is your horse reacting to you?As you approach your horse what do you notice in him? Describe any communication coming from him in the form of body language, posture, positioning, breathing, and expressions. Does he change or stay the same? How do you react to him?

_____

_____

_____

_____

5.   When and how do you greet your horse? When and how does he greet you? How has this changed over the last several sessions?

_____

_____

_____

_____

6.   If there was another level of mindfulness or awareness that you could bring to the approach and greeting of your horse what would it be?

_____

_____

_____

_____

7.   Challenge yourself to engage in that next level and record your experience here.

_____

_____

_____

_____

Step 2: Grooming and preparing

*For additional guidance reference Part 2, Step 2

1.   Does your preparation and location for this step remain the same every session or does it vary? Why or why not?

_____

_____

_____

_____

2.   Take a moment to breathe in synchrony with your horse and then continue that exercise, at intervals if necessary, into grooming and tacking. Describe this experience here. How is it different? Does it benefit you? Your horse? If so, how?

_____

_____

_____

_____

3.   How often do you repeat the mindfulness exercises of noticing your breath and checking in with your 5 senses? What affect does this have on keeping you present and aware of your environment and horse? What other sensations, feelings, emotions, or thought patterns do you notice while checking in with yourself?

_____

_____

_____

_____

4.   While grooming and preparing your horse, what communication(s) do you receive from him in the form of changes in body language, posture, positioning, breathing, and expressions? What is occurring that causes your horse to express this to you? What might he be communicating to you?

_____

_____

_____

_____

5.   At the time of this communication what do you notice in yourself as far as feelings, sensations, emotions, or thoughts? What would you like to do as a result of this communication?

_____

_____

_____

_____

6.   What is your biggest take-away from today's grooming and preparation session?

_____

_____

_____

_____

Step 3: "Mane" event pre-assessment

For more guidance reference Part 2, Step 3

1.   As you make final preparations and adjustments what do you notice about your breath? About your horse's breath? What is registering in each of your 5 senses?

_____

_____

_____

_____

2.   What communications are you getting from your horse as you make final preparations?

_____

_____

_____

_____

3.   Describe your mood, confidence level, emotions, body language, focus, and thoughts. What effect, if any, are these having on your horse?

_____

_____

_____

_____

4.   Observe your horse. Describe his mood, confidence level, emotional state, and focus. Challenge yourself to base these observations on his body language, expression, and posture to avoid projecting.

_____

_____

_____

_____

5.   Based on your observations of your own and your horse's current states of being, what is the next best step to take?

_____

_____

_____

_____

6.   What patterns or correlations are you becoming aware of after several sessions of pre-ride mindfulness practice? How has your pre-ride routine evolved?

_____

_____

_____

_____

7.   What stands out to you the most at this time? What does that tell you about yourself, your horse, or your relationship?

_____

_____

_____

_____

Step 4: "Mane" event

*For additional guidance reference Part 2, Step 4

1.   What method are you using to remind yourself to stay present by noticing your breath and checking in with your 5 senses? How has your ability to stay present in the moment evolved over the last several sessions? How does your horse react when you become present?

_____

_____

_____

_____

2.   Use the following chart to track notable circumstances, changes, or events (positive or negative). With each circumstance note your mood, confidence level, emotions, physical sensations (most notably tension), body language, focus, and thoughts. Also note your horse's mood, confidence level, emotional state, physical qualities (most notably tension), body language, and focus. Then record any correlations or patterns you see developing.

Notable circumstance.	Notes on your mood, confidence level, emotions, physical sensations (most notably tension), body language, focus, and thoughts as this occurs.	Notes on your horse's mood, confidence level, emotional state, physical qualities (most notably tension), body language, and focus as this occurs.	Observations on the relationship between these elements, patterns, and the components that contribute to ease and harmony or tension and imbalance.
1.			
2.			
3.			

Notable circumstance.	Notes on your mood, confidence level, emotions, physical sensations (most notably tension), body language, focus, and thoughts as this occurs.	Notes on your horse's mood, confidence level, emotional state, physical qualities (most notably tension), body language, and focus as this occurs.	Observations on the relationship between these elements, patterns, and the components that contribute to ease and harmony or tension and imbalance.
4.			
5.			
6.			

3.   What stands out to you the most about the notable moments you recorded in the chart?

_____

_____

_____

_____

4.   What went well? What would you like to change or do differently?

_____

_____

_____

_____

5.   If there is something you would like to change or do differently what outcome would you like to experience and what are the steps you can take to affect that outcome?

_____

_____

_____

_____

6. What benefits are mindfulness and increased awareness bringing to you, your horse, and your relationship at this time?

_____

_____

_____

_____

7. If there was another level of mindfulness to bring to your riding what would it be? Challenge yourself to explore that and record your experience here.

_____

_____

_____

_____

8. What is your biggest take-away from your session today?

_____

_____

_____

_____

Step 5: "Mane" Event Post-Assessment

*For additional guidance reference Part 2, Step 5

1.   Describe your present state of being considering your mood, confidence level, emotions, physical sensations, body language, focus, and thoughts. How do these observations compare to your previous ones?

_____

_____

_____

_____

2.   Describe your horse's present state of being considering his mood, confidence level, emotional state, physical qualities, body language, and focus. How do these observations compare to your previous ones?

_____

_____

_____

_____

3.   What patterns or correlations are you noticing at this time?

_____

_____

_____

_____

4.   Breathe in synchrony with your horse. Allow yourself some extra time to explore and track your breath, as well as your sensory and somatic observations. Do they change or stay the same? How do you react to this? How does your horse react? Record your experience here.

_____

_____

_____

_____

5.   How do you thank your horse for his effort and participation during your time together or as you are saying good bye to him? How does he react to this? What is he communicating to you at this time?

_____

_____

_____

_____

6.　What stands out to you, or what is your biggest take-away from today?

_____

_____

_____

_____

Step 6: Life applications

*For additional guidance reference Part 2, Step 6

1.   What have you learned or experienced through these exercises that would be helpful in other areas of your life? Describe the circumstance(s) in which what you've learned would be helpful.

_____

_____

_____

_____

2.   What might the result be of applying what you've learned to this other circumstance?

_____

_____

_____

_____

3.   If you had to pick one application, skill, or exercise that you feel would be easiest to start with to integrate into a situation outside of time spent with your horse, what would it be?

_____

_____

_____

_____

4.   Challenge yourself to commit to applying what you've learned here to some situation outside of being with your horse. Describe that experience and the outcome here.

.

_____

_____

_____

_____

5.   What difference do you notice in yourself after practicing mindfulness in other areas of your life?

_____

_____

_____

_____

6.   What differences do you notice in those around you after practicing mindfulness in other areas of your life? How has the change you've made in yourself rippled out to others connected to you?

_____

_____

_____

_____

About the Author

    Stephanie Sawtelle has had a lifelong affinity for the natural world, especially animals, in particular, horses. Since graduating with a Bachelor of Science degree in Equine Science from Delaware Valley College she has been starting and training horses, and instructing students in horsemanship and riding.

After years of observing the dynamics of the horse-human relationship on the physical, mental, and emotional levels she became interested in the fields of equine facilitated learning (EFL) and equine assisted psychotherapy (EAP) and sought additional training through EAGALA (Equine Assisted Growth and Learning Association). She became an EAGALA Certified Equine Specialist, increasing her skills to include partnering with horses to help people experience profound personal growth and healing.

Seeking to further her expertise in the EFL field she completed a year-long apprenticeship through The Academy for Coaching with Horses to become a Certified Equine-Assisted Life Coach with a focus on the mind-body connection, emotional intelligence, energetic awareness, and intuitive development.

She has developed and facilitated equine-assisted experiential learning sessions, workshops, and classes for a wide variety of clients throughout the United States, and considers it a deep honor and blessing to serve, with the help of the horses themselves, as a guide to others in exploring and elevating the horse-human relationship.